Advance Praise

"This book is ridiculous, which from a Zen perspective is high praise indeed!"

MARK WATTS
filmmaker and archivist of *Out of Your Mind: Essential
Listening from the Alan Watts Audio Archives*

"Every once in a while a book comes
along that will change your life.
While you're waiting, read this one."
Lama Kakha
author of *How to Reincarnate as a Famous Lama*

"Rabbi Rami is a rare sage and trickster rolled into one. With sparkling wit, he demonstrates in this unique book that profound and daring truths are best conveyed through humor and laughter."

IMAM JAMAL RAHMAN
author of *Sacred Laughter of the Sufis*

"Some things are not meant to be known.
This book is full of those things."
Ellen Calhoon
author of *A Luddite's Guide to God*

"Rami Shapiro gets the real secret of religions: at their very heart, the best of them are meant to free us from dogma itself. Here are some great ways of thinking hard, laughing loud, and breaking free that should make any reader—naïve believer or cynical outsider—into a spiritual revolutionary."

DOUGLAS RUSHKOFF
author of *Nothing Sacred: The Truth About Judaism*

"Why did Bodhidharma come from the West? To borrow my copy of this book."

Kung Pao
author of *Take No Ch'ances*

"Wake up! Buckle your seat belt. Be prepared for a raucous ride into the future. With his wit, creative use of language, and a twinkle in his eyes, Rabbi Rami gives name and voice to a movement that has been brewing for a long time. *Holy Rascals* delights and challenges us to open our thinking while we laugh at our own foolishness and gain wisdom in the process. This reverent/irreverent book is filled with practices and memorable stories that support those of us who know we are subversive holy rascals as well as those who will recognize that they too are a member of this tribe. Highly recommended!"

KAY LINDAHL
author of *The Sacred Art of Listening*

"This book is not worth the paper it's printed on, and I bought the Kindle version."

Mandy Montoya
author of *My God, My God, Why Have I Forsaken You: An Atheist's Journey*

"I love this book. I feel at home in it. There isn't a sentence in this book that I don't agree with 150 percent, and it is all presented with an intelligent, sensitive, and brash humor that only slightly veils the sadness over a world so in need of religion and yet ignorant of it. Enjoy the humor, but don't neglect the wisdom that is on every page. Now I hope Rabbi Rami will anoint me in holy rascality."

THOMAS MOORE
author of *Care of the Soul*

"Sure, this book is hilarious. I kept barging into my husband's studio to read him passages of such sublime irreverence they left us both breathless. But it is also terrifyingly pertinent. The vast majority of religious propositions are not only ridiculous, but dangerous. This book pulls back the curtain and exposes the little man who has replaced real magic with fake power. In his fierce truth-telling, Rabbi Rami reconnects the yearnings of our own wild hearts with the sacred soul of the world."

MIRABAI STARR
author of *Caravan of No Despair: A Memoir of Loss and Transformation* and *God of Love: A Guide to the Heart of Judaism, Christianity, and Islam*

"Mystic, scholar, trickster, grenade-roller . . . no one else puts all of these together in one package like Rami Shapiro. If you like fine writing, clear-eyed wisdom, impish irreverence, and compassion for the insanities of the spiritual journey, *Holy Rascals* is for you. After reading *Holy Rascals* you may just conclude, 'Oh, me too! I'm a holy rascal—I just didn't know it until now!'"

GORDON PEERMAN
author of *Blessed Relief: What Christians Can
Learn from Buddhists about Suffering*

"At once side-splittingly hilarious and heartbreakingly on target, this outrageous tour de force of a spiritual manifesto reminds us once again that great irony wielded with great compassion can be a powerful vehicle of truth."

CYNTHIA "MOKSHA" BOURGEAULT
recovering goddess and inter-spiritual incendiary;
author of *The Wisdom Way of Knowing*, *The Heart of
Centering Prayer*, and *Love Is Stronger than Death*

"Truth is one. Different people call it by different names. This isn't one of them."

Sri Sri Sri Sri
author of *Sat, Shit, Ananda: The Yogic Path to Blissful Bowel Movements*

"*Holy Rascals* is at times brilliant, funny, abrasive, and insightful. It poses the big question about religion: Are we making all this up, and if so, how can we make it up in the most positive and life-affirming way? An alternative question might be: Is there a Higher Order Reality that human beings might aspire to, sacrifice for, and be guided by?"

KABIR HELMINSKI
Sufi teacher, translator of Rumi, author of *Living Presence*, *The Knowing Heart*, and *Holistic Islam*

"I'm recommending this book for Banned Books Week."

Rabbi Herschel Ostopol
author of *Choosing Not to Be Chosen: JuBus, HinJews, Jufis, Jewnitarians, and Other Ways to Avoid Going to Shul*

Advice
for SPIRITUAL
Revolutionaries

RAMI SHAPIRO

sounds true
BOULDER, COLORADO

Sounds True
Boulder, CO 80306

Published 2017

Cover design by Lisa Kerans
Book design by Beth Skelley
Cover and interior art by Lisa Kerans

Printed in Canada

Library of Congress Cataloging-in-Publication Data
Names: Shapiro, Rami M., author.
Title: Holy rascals : advice for spiritual revolutionaries /
   by Rabbi Rami Shapiro.
Description: Boulder, CO : Sounds True, 2017. |
   Includes bibliographical references.
Identifiers: LCCN 2017012774 (print) | LCCN 2017039579 (ebook) |
   ISBN 9781622037476 (ebook) | ISBN 9781622037469 (pbk.)
Subjects: LCSH: Religion. | Spirituality. | Shapiro, Rami M.
Classification: LCC BL48 (ebook) | LCC BL48 .S495 2017 (print) |
   DDC 200—dc23
LC record available at https://lccn.loc.gov/2017012774

10 9 8 7 6 5 4 3 2 1

WARNING TO READERS

EVERYTHING IN
THIS BOOK IS TRUE.

LITTLE IF ANYTHING
IS FACT.

To Mack

The turtle who burped and brought Yertle to his knees.

To Toto

Dorothy's dog who pulled the curtain back on the Wizard.

To the Child

Who says what the adults cannot: the emperor has no clothes.

Real religion is the transformation of anxiety into laughter.
Alan Watts

Contents

FOREWORD Analogies Are Spiritual, So Here's One

What helps you find yourself will eventually make you lose yourself, and that's a fact! (In truth, it's just my opinion. But it's a fact that it's my opinion.) Sometimes I drive from my home in Charleston, South Carolina, to visit my family in northwest Ohio. Interstate 75 serves me very well . . . for a while. I'm on it for hours, and it takes me precisely in the direction of my family. Eventually (by *eventually* I mean after many hours of road rage), I get the hell off I-75 because I've arrived at my family's home.

But what if I got attached to the path that was serving me? What if somewhere on my drive, there was a sleight of hand in my consciousness and, without knowing it, I fell more in love with the road than I did my family? "I'm not gonna abandon this road for my family; after all, this road has helped me immensely! It's brought me closer and closer to my family (who I ironically don't care about anymore next to the new sense of belonging I get with the road); it's worked so well for me. Even though I'm in northwest Ohio where I've been aiming all this time, I'm gonna stay on the road and keep going," says my unspoken ego chatter, narrating my attachment. It rambles on, "The road has served me well for a while, so let me make a huge unconscious assumption that it will continue to serve me well for a longer while."

There I'd be trucking along a week later, comforted by the fact that I'm still on the familiar road that I've been on as I'm about to breach northern Canada. (Note: I don't think I-75 goes through northern Canada, but Einstein would be happy if you used the power of your imagination for a moment to pretend that it does.) I'd probably be most comforted by the fact that I *imagine* the road is still serving me well, while in reality (whatever that actually is), it couldn't be dis-serving me more. (The damned road has taken me to the Arctic Circle, and I don't know *any* polar bear self-defense strategies.)

How can the road that leads me to my destination be the same road that leads me away from my destination? (Yes, spiritual folks, I know that *destination* is an unconscious word, as "it's all about the journey." Please shelve the destination dogma for a moment so it doesn't screw up my analogy here. By the way, I've fallen in love with this analogy. I don't want it to end.)

Well, if I were answering my own question (don't mind if I do), I would say, "It's simple physics. It's always that way." When on the road, the relevant questions are, "How long will this road serve me? Can I have the awareness to notice when it's not serving me anymore? And can I have the courage to let go of the road once I realize its service to me has expired?" The path that leads us to our heart will eventually be the path that leads us away from our heart.

Nature seems to teach us this paradoxical lesson everywhere (probably because we've learned really well how not to learn this lesson, #Optimism). The food we eat that nourishes us will also become a source of toxicity if we don't let it go soon enough (that's an implied pooping reference). The landscape is enhanced wonderfully by the rain, but it will also become terrorized by deadly floods if the rain doesn't stop. The turtle is protected being in its shell, but the shell becomes a prison where the turtle will starve if it never comes out. The baby has life because of the womb, and after too many months inside, the same womb would end the baby's life if it didn't move on. (I also have the spiritual talent to drop the caterpillar and butterfly metaphor here, but I feel like we've covered that territory with the turtle and womb metaphors.)

Now to what really counts: let's see if we can put our self-awareness where these words are. What is your road that you're still on, believing that it's serving you because it used to serve you, yet it's no longer serving you? The question isn't, "Do you have your living road metaphor?" I'm going to pretend that you're a human and make the assumption that you do have your version of this. (Tip of the hat to Don Miguel Ruiz. I just made an assumption, and it feels beneficial. Must we make the assumption that assumptions are always bad?) The question is: are you aware of it? Where in your self-identity, thinking, career, relationships, religion, spiritual practice, atheist practice, creativity, or your purpose are you cruising around the Arctic Circle because you stayed on a once-beneficial road for too long?

This is a tough question. (If it wasn't, it probably wouldn't be worth asking and it definitely wouldn't be worth answering.) It suggests that the road we most need to let go of will look like a road we should definitely still be on, at least to our mind. Even if you can't feel exactly what your answer is to this question, would you still be willing to live the adventure of asking yourself the question? And then ask it again, and again, and again, until the question itself becomes a road that no longer serves you?

Laugh or Die Trying Not To

Laughter might be one of the most powerful psychological alchemists we have. To say laughter can be medicinal is an understatement. (I don't know how not to understate it. Perhaps using all caps? LAUGHTER CAN BE MEDICINAL.

Does that feel less understated?) I believe that when we aim laughter correctly, it helps us slice through the scar tissue of our psyche so that we can access something deeper. What is the scar tissue? Old wounds, stories, ways of thinking, certainties, self-identities, resentments, straightjackets of limiting beliefs that bind our gifts, and dogma. What is the "something deeper"? Ways of thinking that serve us better right now, truer senses of self, feelings of purpose, lessons, courage, vulnerability, unleashed gifts, and curiosities. In other words, what lies deeper is likely the stuff that gives us a sense of meaning and inner fulfillment.

The surgeon's scalpel is really effective at cutting, which means it can cut in a way that helps or harms. Where the surgeon aims their scalpel becomes immensely important (I doubt that "aim" is a surgical term taught in medical schools). In the name of slicing through to the treasures that lie deeper within, how can we aim our laughter in a way that truly helps us slice through our psychological scar tissue to allow us to better access the deeper magic? My medically useless yet comedically useful advice is to aim *your* laughter at *your* insecurities, the things that are most important to you, and what offends you the most. In other words, direct it at the things about you that you take so seriously that they seem the most off-limits. If you open the gates of what's most off-limits, you'll likely discover some of your limitlessness (maybe even unlimited amounts of your limitlessness).

The commandment that Moses forgot to write down (understandable, he was getting old) was laugh at thyself. When life challenges us to go deeper into ourselves (it always seems to, damn it!), we can react to it defensively, where we try to escape the challenge through outrage, being offended, adding more concrete certainty to our dogma, victimization, and/or an attitude of preciousness that tells us we're too fragile to be challenged. We can also choose to respond with the courage of an open-hearted warrior who embraces the challenge and therefore goes deeper into themselves. Finding a way to laugh at ourselves—not for the purpose of shaming ourselves, but for the purpose of better understanding ourselves, treating ourselves respectfully rather than seriously, and processing pain rather than avoiding it—aids us well in answering the call to go beyond who we think we are. We're then primed to answer the call to the adventure of realizing a deeper degree of who we really are. (A burning bush told me to write this entire paragraph. #TruthThatYouCantQuestion)

Laugh Your Way Off the Road You Most Travel

What do you call somebody who laughs themselves away from the gravity of certainty and into the levity of curiosity? Somebody who leaves the road they've traveled the most in favor of walking where there's no pavement? Somebody who stops believing their own beliefs? Somebody who betrays the familiar in order to honor the unfamiliar? Somebody who leans away from self-preservation and toward self-realization? Answer: a holy rascal. You're about to go on an adventure with Rami Shapiro where you'll be challenged to be less of what you're not and more of what you are. You'll be challenged to hear less of what you want to hear and more of what you need to hear. With the gift of his hybrid language of insightful humor, my intuition tells me that you'll be entertained while your mind is therapeutically offended.

My intuition is also telling me that your intuition is telling you that *Holy Rascals* is a treasure for helping us all let go of any religion that's deadly to our heart and soul, even though we cling to it as though our life depends on it. This book also works wonders for helping us realize that we turn anything into a religion that we're willing to die for (and oftentimes we do die at some level for it) when we stop questioning it.

I'm delighted for the journey that you're about to go on with Rami Shapiro! Here's to being a holy rascal! Life is a little too short and a lot too important not to be one.

JP Sears
author of *How to Be Ultra Spiritual:*
12½ Steps to Spiritual Superiority

Welcome to the Kali Yuga

Welcome to the Kali Yuga, the moment of civilizational meltdown: the epoch when the long-repressed shadow side of humanity comes once more into its own and our Gods shatter the chains of political correctness imposed upon them by well-meaning liberals hoping to create world peace through an Esperanto-like spirituality.

Authentic spirituality is a sword beaten out of a ploughshare and a spear made out of a pruning hook that pierce the fences of complacency erected to imprison the mind in the mediocre and creativity in the commonplace.

Apocalypse in the rearview mirror is closer than you think.
RR

The Kali Yuga is a time of charlatans masquerading as saints and saints forced to be sinners in order to be saints. And all of them are rascals: some holy, most not.

Religion in the Kali Yuga comes in two flavors: the irrelevant and the irrational. Irrelevant religions focus on pomp but lack all punch: flowing robes, but not flowing passions. Their leaders teach what they have always taught and preach what they have always preached, and

Sticks and stones can break your bones, but beliefs can cut your head off.
RR

no one—not even their teachers and preachers—believes what they are saying. Their religion is simply about saying it. So they read the old words without new understandings and wonder why so few take them seriously.

Religion is what keeps the poor from murdering the rich.
Napoleon Bonaparte

It does so by convincing the poor to murder each other.
RR

Irrational religions are where the passion is. Maybe where it has always been. People love irrationality; this is what separates us from the rest of the animal kingdom. The irrational religions imagine a once-upon-a-time Golden Age and seek to rebuild it in the present. They celebrate a time when men were men and Gods were Gods and both got to impregnate or kill whomever they wanted; a time before science, Seinfeld, Stewart, and the Nineteenth Amendment to the US Constitution; a time when story was history, and myth was fact, and Gods were real, and their spokesmen (the Gods almost always spoke through men) had the power to wage war, strike fear, control women, and amass great wealth. And so these passionate lovers of a romanticized past seek to reestablish their caliphates and rebuild their temples and make sure that Adam never marries Steve and Eve is forced to use the bathroom the Good Lord intended her to use.

Here's the good news: civilization is a product of our imagination. Politics, religion, economics, music, art, dance, literature—they are all products of our imagination. That's good news because if civilization is a product of our imagination and things aren't going so well, we can imagine something better.

Here's the bad news: the Kali Yuga is a time of imagination malfunction, when we cannot imagine better, or those who can imagine better are so few in number as to be rendered impotent. Imagination needs to reach critical mass if it is to shape civilization, and at this Kali Yuga moment, critical mass lies with dystopian fantasies rooted in tribalism, terror, death of neighbors, and destruction of nature.

Of course there are exceptions, but focusing on exceptions only blinds us to the rule. To pretend that we all worship the same God and that religion is all about love and peace is to ignore our competing and mutually exclusive theologies and deny our complicity in the oppression, exploitation, and murder of tens—if not hundreds—of thousands in the name of religion in this life and in the torture of millions more in our fantasies of eternal damnation in the next.

Those who believe absurdities will commit atrocities.
Voltaire

The Kali Yuga must run its course. But even if we can't win, we can resist. Resistance is the prophetic spirituality of the Kali Yuga.

> While the neutral observer may see all religions as being similar, adherents see them as categorically different and incompatible. My religion is the true one. The others are the work of Satan: falsehoods designed to trap the unwary. Believers cannot compare religions in the way they compare cars because to the extent that they believe in one religion, the others are not viable alternatives.
>
> STEVE BRUCE, in *Religions as Brands*

Holy rascals are the shock troops of the resistance, and their weapon is humor. While they may not be able to muster the critical mass needed to imagine new Gods, they can reveal the absurdity of the Gods we have. If enough people can be empowered to laugh at the Great and Terrible Wizard, if enough people can be empowered to laugh at the pious Yertles who have built their towers of power on their backs, and if enough people can be empowered to laugh at the nakedness of those who wrap themselves in illusion, we can weaken the impact of our psychopathic Gods and their (our) homicidal fantasies and prepare ourselves to imagine something better when the Kali Yuga passes.

If you do not resist the apparently inevitable, you will never know how inevitable the inevitable was.
Terry Eagleton,
Why Marx Was Right

The path of the holy rascal is the path of greatest resistance. To resist is to sist again and again. To sist, from the Latin *sistere*, means "to stand and to assist others to stand." The holy rascal's task is to stand against the madness that passes for religion and to assist others in doing the same.

This book invites you to resist the horror of the Kali Yuga by laughing your ass off when called upon to cut your neighbor's head off. Humor is the one thing Gods and clergy cannot fight. It is the one thing they fear the most. The surest way to slay a God is to laugh at the madness the God promotes. This is what holy rascals are called to do, and this book is a manifesto and guide to doing it.

Swami Vas iz Das
Vedanta Center
Del Boca Vista, Florida
May 2017

Introduction

This book is an act of holy rascality. It isn't well reasoned, well argued, or even well thought out. It is simply an exercise in truth telling.

The book is divided into three parts. The first, "The Mind of a Rascal: An Unauthorized Autobiography," offers a glimpse into my personal path to holy rascality. The second, "Religion Unveiled: The Tao of Toto," is a holy rascal-esque look at different aspects of religion and spirituality. The third, "Hacking the Holy," shares the primary tools of spiritual culture jamming and invites you to get in the game of holy rascality. The book closes with an epilogue titled "There's a God at the End of This Book!," an example of holy rascality.

Because the art of holy rascality relies heavily on short writing, most "chapters" are brief, with each one asserting its point rather than arguing on its behalf. In this way you are invited to say yes or no to each point without overthinking it. If you say yes, you are rewarded with a quick hit of endorphins. If you say no, you suffer pangs of buyer's remorse.

To save you time, here are the underlying assumptions of this book:

1 Brand-name parochial religions are concerned with their respective truths rather than the Perennial Wisdom at the mystic heart of all religion.

2 Knowing this allows you to learn from and even participate in all religions without becoming trapped in any of them.

3 Those who hold the copyright to brand-name religions don't want you to know this.

4 Holy rascals do.

5 The best way to free religion from the parochial and for the perennial is humor.

Now that you no longer have to wonder what this book is about, you are free to read it just for fun. After all, that's why I wrote it.

The mind of a
RASCAL
an unauthorized
autobiography

Truth is one.
Different people call it by different names.
All of them are wrong.

RR

1

PROLOGUE   A Holy Rascal Manifesto

Religiosity is the human capacity for making meaning out of
the raw facts of human existence. Brand-name religions have
abandoned the making in order to worship the made. While
religion at its best calls us to a community of the curious and
a unity beyond dogma and tribalism, religion at its worst calls
us to worship the very things that divide us and to pit people
against one another in the name of one fantasy or other.

Using humor, play, and fearless joy, holy rascals free people
from idolatry and open them to the creative art of meaning
making at the heart of human religiosity. In so doing we free
brand-name religions from the madness that robs them of
creativity and meaning as well.

We welcome all religious teachings that promote dignity,
justice, compassion, humility, respect, awe, and love for all
beings. We reject all religious teachings that promote fear,
hatred, and the exploitation
or demonization of the other.
And we shun all Gods who
sanction violence in this
world or the next.

*The God© who can be branded
is not the Eternal God.
The same is true of the God©
who can be copyrighted.*
RR

We call upon peoples
of every religion to cleanse
their texts and teachings of violence,
injustice, and hatred; to boldly speak out when their religion is
hijacked by evil; and to continually move their religion beyond
the zero-sum world view of us *against* them and toward the
nonzero world view of all of us together.

2

INTERVIEW WITH A RASCAL
AltGuru Talks with Rabbi Rami

AltGuru Should I call you His Holy Rascalness Rabbi Rami?
Rabbi Rami Rabbi Rami is fine. I only use that title for
state dinners.

AG And how often does that happen?
RR Never, but I like to be prepared. I was lecturing in New
Delhi with His Holiness the Fourteenth Dalai Lama, who,
by the way, is not my favorite: when it comes to Dalai
Lamas and Doctors Who, I prefer the Ninth, and I was
tempted to have myself introduced in a similar fashion,
but then I considered the bad karma that might accrue
and went with Rabbi Rami instead.

AG Do you believe in karma?
RR No, but I could be wrong. That's why I'm ready to join
every religion on the off chance that one of them might
be right.

AG Where's the integrity in that?
RR Integrity? I just want to be on the winning team. I don't
want to be burning in hell and have the guy burning
next to me lean over and say, "Well, at least we have our
integrity." Screw integrity! I want the brass ring.

AG And the brass ring is?
RR Heaven, Nirvana, the Pure Land, salvation, reincarnation
as a rich guy—all the marketing promises religions make
to entice me to join and convince me to pay.

> Karma is the invention of the powerful
> used to explain to the powerless why
> they are not among the powerful.
>
> **RR**

AG There are so many competing rings; which one do
you pursue?

RR I pursue the ones that agree with me.

AG So you are the final arbiter of truth?

RR Of course. If you believe in "this" and not "that," it is
because, for whatever reason, "this" makes more sense
to you than "that." There is no way to know you're right;
you just follow your gut or your conditioning and then
deny you are doing so in order to pretend you are not the
final arbiter of truth. But you are. There's no escaping it.

AG Is there no such thing as Truth with a capital T?

RR I think there is, but I don't think it can be put into words
and marketed to us as a "this" or a "that." You come to
Truth when you free yourself from "this" and "that." And
once you're free from "this" and "that," you're free to play
with "this" and "that" for the sheer joy of playing. This is
what Ch'an Master Seng-Ts'an meant when he said, "Seek
not after Truth; cease only to cherish opinions." Free
yourself from the truth claims of religion and see the
Truth to which no religion can lay claim.

AG Where did the term *holy rascal* come from?

RR From Sister Jose Hobday, a Seneca elder and Franciscan
nun. After listening to a talk I gave at the Aspen Chapel
in Aspen, Colorado, Sister Jose called out, "He's a holy
rascal!" It stuck.

AG   Do you know what she meant by it?

RR   Holy rascals use the language of the holy—religious language, spiritual language—to unmask the absurdities of religion and spirituality. Holy rascals aren't against religion; we only want people to see religion for what it is—a cultural construct—rather than what religions claim to be—absolute Truth.

AG   What does it mean that religions are cultural constructs?

RR   All religions are human narratives carrying the memes and metaphors we use to create meaning out of the raw facts of our existence. We are meaning-making animals. Religion is a vehicle for creating, preserving, and perpetuating meaning.

AG   So religions aren't true?

RR   Religions carry Truth the way a thermos carries coffee. You drink from a thermos; you don't drink the thermos itself.

AG   Yet religions claim to be true.

RR   Yes, and often exclusively so. For example, Jesus teaches the Golden Rule (Matthew 7:12; Luke 6:31), a teaching common to all religions, but it is Jesus's divinity and not the Golden Rule that defines Christianity's claim to being true. If it were the rule, Christianity couldn't claim superiority over any other religion that teaches the rule.

Religions go bad when the search for Truth is replaced by the preservation of power.
RR

> When I compare wash powders Sudso and Osdus, I suppose
> that I am comparing similar chemicals and that my choice
> of one over the other could easily be reversed. . . . [This
> is not the case with religion.] The Muslim does not view
> Christianity as a very similar product that with a bit of
> tweaking could be every bit as attractive. . . . The religion
> to which one adheres is the truth; the religion one rejects
> is the world of the devil.
>
> STEVE BRUCE, in *Religions as Brands*

AG Is the religion of the holy rascal true?

RR Holy rascality isn't a religion, and holy rascals come
from all religions and none. While we have no official
theology, we are drawn to the Perennial Wisdom at the
mystic heart of all religions: All is God, Brahman, Reality,
Universe, the Mother, the Absolute, however named; you
can know Reality directly; knowing Reality leads to living
justly, kindly, and for the benefit of all; and knowing
Reality and living justly, kindly, and for the benefit of all
is the true calling of humanity. Our task is to free religion
from the parochial and irrational and for the perennial
and sane.

Toto,
I've a feeling we're not
in Kansas anymore.
Dorothy

AG So Abraham, Moses, Jesus, and Buddha are fictional characters?

RR Almost certainly. While I don't doubt that Jesus was a historical figure, the Jesus we know from Saint Paul and the authors of the Gospels is the creation of Saint Paul and the authors of the Gospels. Jesus of Nazareth is not nearly as important as Jesus of narrative. Does it really matter whether Jesus or the Buddha preached the teachings attributed to them? Not at all; it is the wisdom in the teachings that matter, not their historicity.

AG So holy rascals are the exposers of stories?

RR Holy rascals are spiritual culture jammers who use humor, play, creativity, and critical thinking to reveal the human origins of religions and how religions mask their true origins behind the conceit of divine origins. Religion is a human construct for the creation, preservation, and perpetuation of meaning and meaning making. Sometimes religion becomes corrupted into fear-based systems of control that promote enmity between people and the economic and political elevation of a privileged religious, financial, political, and military class. Holy rascals pull back the curtain on that ruling class to free people from blindly following them. We want people to know that the "divine" behind the "divine right of kings" is simply a puppet of the kings themselves.

> Sweetheart, even Kansas isn't in Kansas anymore.
> **Toto**

> Once you realize that every religion is using the same claim as Coke— "It's the real thing"—you cannot help but realize that, like Coke, every religion is filled with fizz.
>
> **RR**

AG Holy rascals reveal the emperor has no clothes, then.

RR Absolutely. Without clothes, the emperor is no longer emperor. The clothes are the stories the emperor tells in order to justify being emperor. This works only if the emperor can convince us that these stories are really histories. Holy rascals examine these stories to reveal the constructed nature of the emperor's power and use humor to free people from stories that no longer serve a universal quest for global justice, compassion, and meaning.

AG What do you mean by "brand-name religions"?

RR A brand is a story developed for a specific product that distinguishes it from similar products. A brand-name religion is a religion whose story distinguishes it from other religions. The Jewish brand is "We are God's Chosen People." The Muslim brand is "We've got God's final Prophet and uncorrupted Revelation." Every clergyperson is marketing a brand. That's why a Methodist can no more discover that Krishna is Christ than the marketers of Coke can discover that Pepsi is "the Real Thing" or than the marketers of Pepsi can discover that Coke is "the Choice of a New Generation."

AG Are you saying religion is the same as Coke and Pepsi?

RR Like religion, Coke and Pepsi compete against
each other over story, market share, and shelf space,
but—and here is where religion differs from other
products—the good people at Coca-Cola don't seek to
keep Coke drinkers from marrying Pepsi drinkers, and
the good people at Pepsi have yet to declare jihad on
those of us who prefer Coke, and neither imagines the
other will burn in hell for their soft drink preference.
Of course, I can't speak for Dr. Pepper.

> There can be no doubt that *branding as a concept* is
> applicable to religious phenomenon. Religions . . . have
> brand names: Christianity, Islam, Judaism, or Christian
> Science. They normally have . . . easily recognizable *brand
> logos*: the cross or fish for Christianity, the Yin-Yang for
> Taoism, the star and crescent for Islam, the Lotus flower for
> Buddhism, the star of David for Judaism. They have "brand
> stories" (myths) that are embodied in rituals, objects, works
> of art, buildings, and clothing.
>
> JÖRG STOLZ AND JEAN-CLAUDE USUNIER,
> in *Religions as Brands*

AG   What about clergy? Do we really need them?

RR   Sure, but to see why, let me change analogies for a second. Clergy are like Dungeon Masters in the Dungeons & Dragons role-playing game. If you want to play the game, you need a Dungeon Master to weave the story. If you want to play the game called Catholic Mass, for example, you need Catholic priests to literally turn wafer and wine into the body and blood of Christ. No one else can do that. So Catholic priests are essential to the Catholic game. The same is true of other clergy in the context of their games.

AG   Calling religion a game seems demeaning.

RR   All life is a game or a complex of games, so the issue isn't game or no game, but what kind of game you are playing. There are two kinds of games: finite zero-sum games and infinite nonzero games. The goal of finite zero-sum games is to win at the expense of the other. Tennis, for example, is a finite zero-sum game. The goal is to end the game by defeating your opponent. The goal of infinite nonzero games is to keep the game going. Playing rather than winning is the point. Friendship is an example of an infinite game. The goal of friendship is to keep the friendship going, not to end the friendship with one friend winning at the expense of the other.

If the concept of God has any validity or any use,
it can only be to make us larger, freer, and more loving.
If God cannot do this, then it is time we got rid of Him.
James Baldwin, *The Fire Next Time*

Religious leaders face the sort of challenge familiar to
cigarette manufacturers. It is not enough to show that their
product is good . . . the brand manager much overcome
some resistance to the kind of thing it is. Fairly or unfairly,
religion has come to be associated with a number of
unpopular things: American politicians, preachy morality,
hypocrisy, child abuse, Islamist extremism, immigrants.
Deinstitutionalized spirituality might be seen as an
attempt to rebrand religious experience by cutting it free
of negative connotations of "religion."

DAVID VOAS, in *Religions as Brands*

AG Which game does religion play?

RR Religion can be played as either. When played as a finite
zero-sum game, religion is all about winning and losing,
with the in-group triumphing over the out-group, if
not in this life, then in the afterlife. When played as
an infinite nonzero game, religion is about seeing the
thriving of all as key to the thriving of each. Holy rascals
try to shift the terms of play from finite zero-sum games
to infinite nonzero games. Shifting to infinite nonzero
games frees brand-name religions from the burden
of Truth. We aren't trying to destroy religion but to
liberate it to do what religion is meant to do—create
meaning—rather than what religion too often tries to
do—monopolize Truth and power.

AG Of course, millions of believers like to play hate-filled games.

RR I don't believe that. Millions of believers participate in hate-filled, fear-driven, finite zero-sum games, but they don't know they are playing a game. They've been convinced that their story is history, that Coke is true and Pepsi is false, and—worse—that Pepsi is the beverage of the Devil. Once they see that this is all a game, and a hurtful one at that, they will stop playing. People don't want to hate; they are simply conditioned to believe that God wants them to hate.

> We are born with a capacity for love and fear; we are not born with a capacity to hate. Hate is something we are taught.
>
> At its best religion builds on love to cultivate compassion and builds on fear to cultivate awe.
>
> At its worst religion builds on love to cultivate jealousy and builds on fear to cultivate hate.   RR

AG Do you ever envision the end of religion?

RR No. While any given brand-name religion can die, people are inherently religious, and religion itself won't disappear. Holy rascals aren't working to end religion; we are working to shift religion from zero-sum to nonzero, from the parochial to the perennial, from fear to love, and from injustice to justice.

AG What do you envision?

RR I can't predict the future, but what I see happening in the present is the emergence of a new seeker class: spiritually independent people willing to cross the boundaries of religious brands in search of Perennial Wisdom, narratives that give their lives meaning, and practices that bring that meaning alive in their lives.

AG And where are the holy rascals among them?

RR We are behind them pushing, we are ahead of them pulling, we are on the sidelines cheering, and we are among them struggling.

AltGuru is the author of Indra's Net: How to be Knotty and Nice. *She currently resides in the Witness Protection Program in the American Southwest.*

3
The Making of a Holy Rascal

I grew up in an Orthodox Jewish home. Basically this meant that my dad went to shul each morning; we didn't eat pork; we separated dairy and meat and so had more pots, pans, dishes, cups, and silverware than the local five and dime store; my mom, sister, and grandmothers always prayed upstairs in our community's huge domed synagogue; and our living room furniture was covered in plastic. With the exception of the last item, our rabbis dictated all these things. Hitler had something to do with the plastic: "You never know when you have to pack up and run away in a hurry" is how it was explained to me. Since running away with your living room furniture makes no sense if the Nazis are coming, I assume the plastic was for the benefit of the anti-Semites who would occupy our house: even Jew haters appreciate a clean couch.

> Thou shalt not cover thy furniture in plastic until thou
> hast invented air conditioning, lest thy thighs stick to it
> in the summer and make a farting sound when getting up.
> THE SECRET BOOK OF LEVITICUS 28:3

The Religions of Man

Two of my high school teachers, Peter Santos and Michael Gelinas, spent the summer before my junior year in India. They came back and taught a class called World Religions, based on Huston Smith's book *The Religions of Man*. (Today the book is published as *The World's Religions*.) I took the course and fell in love with religion, all religions, but especially Advaita Vedanta Hinduism and Zen Buddhism. Two things drew me to these religions: the absence of a personal deity and meditation as a way of testing the truth claims each religion made.

In the old days, you could test the truth claims of Judaism by the weather. God said if you obey his commandments, he will send you rain in its proper seasons so that your harvests will be bountiful and your cattle will be fat (Deuteronomy 11:13–14). When people noticed the weather wasn't matching their piety, their leaders borrowed the idea of an afterlife from the Zoroastrians. "Did we say 'weather'? No, we said 'whether': whether or not you get into heaven." You can't really test the truth claims after you die. By the time you could discover they are false, there is no you left to discover they are false.

> Twenty-five hundred years ago it took an exceptional man like Diogenes to exclaim, "I am not an Athenian or a Greek but a citizen of the world." Today we must all be struggling to make those words our own. We have come to the point in history when anyone who is only Japanese or American, only Oriental or Occidental, is only half human. The other half that beats with the pulse of all humanity has yet to be born.
>
> HUSTON SMITH, *The World's Religions*

I Coulda Been a Messiah

When I was sixteen, my mother came into my room one night around midnight, sat next to me on my bed, and in all sincerity asked me if I were the Messiah. It was the only way she could make sense of my passion for religion. When I said I wasn't, she cried. Then I cried. She cried because this meant we had to wait a bit longer for the Messiah to arrive. I cried because she cried. Also because—now that she mentioned it—it would have been cool to be the Messiah, and since I wasn't and didn't have the forethought to lie about it, I never would be.

> The Messiah will come as soon as the most unbridled individualism of faith becomes possible—when there is no one to destroy this possibility and no one to suffer its destruction. . . . The Messiah will come only when he is no longer necessary; he will come only on the day after his arrival; he will come, not on the last day, but on the very last.
>
> FRANZ KAFKA, *Parable and Paradox*

Sometimes You Just Have to Sleep

The United States bombed Cambodia during the second semester of my freshman year of college. Student protest led to the canceling of classes and final exams. The university invited students to organize their own classes for a week before sending us all home. I organized a morning of meditation. I secured the room, found a professor who could teach the class, and settled in among the hundreds of people who attended.

Sitting in front of me was a very thin and wizened old lady. When the bell sounded the start of meditation, she slipped off her cushion, tucked it under her head, and went to sleep. I spent the next forty minutes making fun of her in my mind. When the bell rang signaling the end of the session, she sat up, turned to face me, and said with a smile, "Sometimes you just have to sleep."

> In the beginning, according to the sages of ancient China, was Flow—Rhythm, Tao, Process. . . . In the beginning, according to the ancient Hebrews, *Ruach*, divine Wind-Breath-Spirit brooded over the formless Deep and breathed it into form. In the beginning, according to both traditions, was rhythmic interplay. Out of this movement came form.
>
> TERESINA HAVENS, *Mind What Stirs in Your Heart*

Jewish Mother Goddess

Her name was Teresina Havens. She was a retired professor of world religion at Smith College. We talked for a long time after the meditation class ended, and I accepted her invitation to meet weekly for a year to study the Bhagavad Gita and the figure of the Divine Mother in Hinduism and Judaism. I had no idea Judaism had a Goddess but found myself gravitating toward her in her many forms: Chochmah/Wisdom, Shechinah/the Divine Presence, Torah, Mishnah, Shabbat, and the five levels of consciousness—Nefesh, Ruach, Neshamah, Chayyah, and Yechidah, or body, heart, mind, soul, and spirit.

Goddesses are ubiquitous.
Raphael Patai,
The Hebrew Goddess

Black Hats, Black Robes

I spent my sophomore year of college at Tel Aviv University studying Jewish mysticism and hanging out with Rabbi Reuven, a mad Kabbalist in his forties who was building a kibbutz for American Jews in hopes of keeping us from becoming American Buddhists. I dressed like a Hasid—black coat, black pants, white shirt, black Borsalino fedora—and spent time at the kibbutz digging in fields both literal and allegorical.

It was Rabbi Reuven who was the first to tell me I was a poet. Sadly, my poetry sounded more Buddhist than Jewish. I told him I longed for the anarchic Hasidism imagined by Martin Buber: all stories, few obligations. He was appalled.

When I returned to the States I studied Buddhism full-time at Smith College with Taitetsu Unno. I told him I longed for the anarchic Buddhism imagined by Alan Watts. He too was appalled.

> I do not accept any absolute formulas for living.
> No preconceived code can see ahead to everything that
> can happen in a man's life. As we live, we grow and
> our beliefs change. They must change. So I think we
> should live with this constant discovery. We should
> be open to this adventure in heightened awareness
> of living. We should stake our whole existence on our
> willingness to explore and experience.
>
> MARTIN BUBER,
> in Kenneth Kramer's *Learning through Dialogue*

Where Is God?

Joshu Sasaki Roshi gave me my first koan, a Zen puzzle designed to crack open my everyday mind so I could experience everyday life with my Everyday Mind. Capital letters make all the difference when it comes to spirituality.

> Enlightenment? I don't like the subject at all.
> **Joshu Sasaki Roshi**[1]

Sitting across from me during a private interview (*dokusan*) at a Zen retreat (*sesshin*), Roshi repeatedly struck the hardwood floor with a gnarled wooden stick while asking, "Where is God when stick hit floor?" He sent me to my meditation cushion to find out.

Periodically Roshi rang a bell announcing, "The Roshi is in," inviting us to share with him our answers to the various koans he assigned. Eventually, after several failed attempts, I came up with a clever answer. As I sat in front of him, our knees almost touching, I grabbed the stick before it struck the floor, intending to pull it from his hand and shout, "No stick! No floor! Just God!" Sadly, I hadn't counted on Roshi not relinquishing the stick. I pulled, he pulled harder, and I went flying onto my back: no stick, all floor, no God. Clever is never good in Zen.

A C in Enlightenment

I quit Zen at that moment, but when the next round of dokusan came up, I blacked out and came to once again sitting on my knees directly in front of Roshi. All I remember was seeing the stick about to strike the floor; then I blacked

19

out again. I can only reconstruct what happened from the position in which I found myself after it happened. I was lying flat out on the floor, face down, my arms extended over my head, my hands clasped together in a ball, and my words ringing in my ears: "GOD IS HERE!" I had become the stick. I hit the floor. And I knew, as they say in Japanese, *Alles iz Gott*, "All is God."

If anyone were to appear and say, Zen Buddhism is Number One! Zen Buddhism is the best! They would be just as bad as everybody else.
Joshu Sasaki Roshi[2]

Roshi laughed. I was impressed. I was certain I was about to be made a roshi in my own right. Roshi stopped laughing. "Good answer," he said. "Seventy-five percent. More zazen!"

Zen Rabbi

Roshi took me aside one day, backed me up against a wall, and demanded that if I wanted to study Zen I must move to Mount Baldy where his monastery was outside Los Angeles, learn Japanese, and sit zazen (meditation). For some reason the thought horrified me. Without thinking I blurted, "Roshi, I can't do that—I'm going to become a rabbi!" That was news to both of us. "Ah," Roshi sighed, smiling, "be rabbi, be Zen rabbi."

Many years latter I learned that Roshi had acted inappropriately with more than a few women students. While this saddened me, it didn't make his teaching any less important to me. I don't have a problem with my teachers being broken; I only wish they wouldn't break their students as a result of it.

A Zen rabbi is like a Zen roshi in that she can do with a Torah scroll what a Zen roshi does with a wooden statue of the Buddha—toss it into a raging fire.

Except she doesn't.

Because she knows a Torah scroll costs way more to replace than a wooden statue of the Buddha.　RR

No One Can Read the Bible but Me

During my first year of rabbinical training in Jerusalem, I attended Rabbi Mordecai Kaplan's ninety-ninth birthday celebration at his synagogue, Kehillat Mevakshei Derech. My master's thesis was on Rabbi Kaplan, the founder of the Reconstructionist movement in Judaism, and I gifted him a copy of it. He accepted the bound thesis graciously and invited me to meet with him at his home the following Wednesday.

As we sat making small talk in his living room, Rabbi Kaplan asked me to take a large print Hebrew-English Bible down from a shelf and read a passage from the prophet Jeremiah. My Hebrew was rough, and I did so haltingly. Kaplan was incensed: "If you can't read Hebrew, you can't be a rabbi. Read it again!" And again, and again, and over and over again until I knew it by heart, but still he was dissatisfied. "Read it in English!" I did. "You can't even read English! Give me the text." I did. And then he read both the Hebrew and the English in a manner that altered the meaning of the text completely. Then he laughed. "Don't worry. No one can read the Bible but me!"

I continued to meet with him regularly throughout that year.

The traditional conception of God is challenged by history, anthropology and psychology; these prove that beliefs similar to those found in the Bible about God arise among all peoples at a certain stage of mental and social development, and pass through a process of evolution which is entirely conditioned by the development of the other elements in their civilization.

MORDECAI KAPLAN, *Judaism as a Civilization*

Unity Principle

My mentor at Hebrew Union College–Jewish Institute of Religion was Dr. Ellis Rivkin. I attended his lecture series in Jerusalem, where he set forth his thesis that at the heart of all things Jewish was a single archetype: unity. Everything was a part of this One Thing some call God, and Judaism was a several-thousand-year-old effort to bring that message to the world. It wasn't that God was one, but that God was Oneness itself. The stick had just hit the bimah!*

The traditional conception of God is an idea whose time has gone. RR

---

*The elevated platform in the synagogue from which the rabbi and cantor lead services.

The unity principle has to be distinguished from the changing concepts of God, for the latter are the solutions to the specific problems within the historical continuum which may have a limited and temporal quality, whereas the unity principle is an eternal quality.

ELLIS RIVKIN, *The Dynamics of Jewish History*

I, Megalomaniac

It became clear to the leadership at Hebrew Union College–
Jewish Institute of Religion that my nondual theology didn't
fit well with the conventional dualism of Reform Judaism.
After giving a talk on nondualism during a Shabbat service
at the college, I was called into the dean's office.

"You are a megalomaniac," the rabbi said angrily.

"Oh, no sir, I'm not," I replied flatly. "A megalomaniac
thinks he's God. I know I'm God."

> Behold you are God and God is you; for you
> are so intimately one with God that you
> cannot by any means be separate from God,
> for you are God. See now that I, even I, am
> God. God is I and I am God.
>
> ABRAHAM ABULAFIA[3]

Rejection

I first learned of Reb Zalman Schachter-Shalomi, the
founder of Jewish Renewal, in the late seventies, when I
read his doctoral thesis on Hasidic counseling techniques.
After I moved to Miami, I discovered that Reb Zalman
spent a week each year offering classes to local rabbis. It
was love at first sight.

After a few years of study, Reb Zalman and I were
walking in my Miami neighborhood just after Hanukkah.
I asked him to stop and formally requested he take me on
as a disciple, a Hasid. He refused. Thinking this was a test
of my sincerity, I asked several more times. The answer was
always the same.

Eventually Reb Zalman took pity on me and said, "Rami-*libn* [Rami dearest], you don't understand our relationship. Sometimes I will be your rebbe. And sometimes you will be my rebbe."

He was right. I didn't understand.

> Do not exalt any path above God. There are many paths that lead to God.
>
> So people are capable of finding and following the ways that suit them, provided they do not stand still.
>
> ZALMAN SCHACHTER-SHALOMI,
> *Wrapped in a Holy Flame*

I, Rebbe

I continued to study with Reb Zalman for more than two decades.

During a week-long retreat with Reb Zalman at the original Elat Chayyim Jewish Renewal retreat center in upstate New York, he sent one of his Hasidim to tell me to be at the rebbe's cabin the following morning at six.

Reb Zalman waved me into his living room and onto a chair. He was on the phone talking to one of his children in Israel. When he hung up he sat next to me and said, "Do you remember twenty years ago, when you asked to be my Hasid and I said no?" I nodded. "Remember I said sometimes I'd be your rebbe and sometimes you'd be mine?" I nodded. "Now is that time."

He reached behind a chair and pulled out two beautiful handwritten parchments. The first formally added Reb Zalman's name to my original rabbinic ordination. The second proclaimed me a rebbe in his lineage. Pulling me to my feet, he embraced me and recited the names of his rebbes, beginning with the Baal Shem Tov, the founder of Hasidism in the eighteenth century. He then added his name to the chain and mine right after it.

He spent the next hour explaining to me the mystic significance of this event, but by then I was sobbing so intensely I had no idea what he said.

It Doesn't Work

During this time I continued my daily zazen. Still, no enlightenment. I called Rev. Taitetsu Unno, my Buddhist professor at Smith College, to complain. He invited me to meet with him at his home in Northampton, Massachusetts. When we did he said simply, "It doesn't work."

There is nothing you can do to achieve Nirvana, he explained. It is a matter of grace. Sit because you like sitting. Or quit because you don't like sitting. But don't sit for any reason other than to sit.

Today I still sit, but only because I like sitting. Enlightenment is a young person's game.

The Return of the Mother

I had my first vision of Mother Mary while living in Miami. I saw her in a photograph of an oil slick on a bank window in Clearwater, Florida. I saw her many times after that. Sometimes she was Mary; sometimes she was Kali; sometimes she was Chochma.

Once, while walking before dawn in Lithia Park in Ashland, Oregon, she taught me a mantra I have recited daily for the past quarter century.

Years later, while chanting the Ave Maria at 2:00 a.m. before a statue of Our Lady of Guadalupe at La Casa de Maria in Santa Barbara, California, she spoke to me. "Do you know why I'm called the Perpetual Virgin?" she asked.

"No," I said.

"I'm called the Perpetual Virgin because I am the mother of all living things, and I am so in love with each that it is as if there were none else. Each birth is my first and only."

Hail Mary,
full of grace.
The Happening
of all happening
is with you.
And with the rest of us
as well.   RR

The Mother's Searing Love

Having visions of the Divine Mother is not a job description for rabbis, so I sought advice on how to put an end to these experiences from my friend and teacher Andrew Harvey, one of the world's great mystics and a devotee of the Divine Mother. We sat together in the Phoenix airport, and I explained my dilemma. In his delightfully boisterous and hyperdramatic way, Andrew explained to me (and everyone within three gates of us on either side) that the Divine Mother would shatter all I hold dear, strip me naked of all beliefs, and send me tumbling madly into bottomless free fall until I finally learned to live without surety, certainty, security, and knowing, at which point the falling wouldn't cease but my fear of hitting bottom would.

There is no bottom when falling into Mother's searing love.

> We are now, I believe, on the threshold of a third stage [of spiritual evolution] which I call the stage of the sacred marriage. This is the only position we could possibly take and still survive. This is a stage beyond both matriarchy and patriarchy. . . . Not only should we invoke the sacred feminine, restore the sacred feminine, but this union between the matriarchal and the patriarchal, the sacred marriage, must be accomplished in the spirit of the sacred feminine for it to be real, effective, rich, and fecund. It must occur in her spirit of unconditional love, in her spirit of tolerance, forgiveness, all-embracing and all-harmonizing balance, and not, in any sense, involve a swing in the other direction.
>
> ANDREW HARVEY, *The Return of the Mother*

My Priest

In 1984 Father Thomas Keating, one of the founders of the Centering Prayer movement, invited me to attend the first gathering of what was to become a three-decade-long conversation among contemplatives from different religions held at St. Benedict's Monastery in Snowmass, Colorado. There was just one rule at the Snowmass Group: you may speak only from your experience with contemplative practice. While you may use the *language* of your tradition, you must not speak *for* your tradition. Within the first three days, it became clear to me that while our methods and languages differed, our experience was the same: we each slipped beyond self into Self, beyond the sense that we are apart from God to a realization that we are a part of God.

I last visited with Father Thomas in the summer of 2016. He was very frail. "How are you preparing for death?" I asked him.

"The same way I lived my life: by emptying myself of Thomas moment to moment."

"And where do you imagine you will go when you die?"

"When there is no you, there is nowhere for you to go."

For human beings, the most daunting challenge is to become fully human. For to become fully human is to become fully divine.

Thomas Keating, *Manifesting God*

Daughters of Wisdom

In the summer of 2001, I visited the Daughters of Wisdom in Litchfield, Connecticut. I asked Sisters Rosemarie and Jo-Ann to show me their chapel. The room was simple, with a beautiful stone altar, but over the altar, where I had expected to see a crucifix, was a life-sized gray concrete statue of Mary, her feet on the moon, her hands folded in a *namaste* gesture, seeming to float out over the congregation. Looking at the Mother, I felt an unshakable presence of compassion and peace.

"Where's Jesus?" I asked. Sister Rosemarie opened a small drawer in a wooden chest and pulled out a brass crucifix. "We only bring him out when Father comes to say Mass."

The Daughters of Wisdom is a Catholic order founded in 1704 by Saint Louis Marie de Montfort and Sister Marie Louise Trichet, and devoted to the study of the Wisdom Literature of the Bible: Proverbs, Job, Ecclesiastes, Sirach, and the Wisdom of Solomon. Under the guidance of these wonderful women, these books became my primary Torah.

> God wants you to become holy . . . dust into
> light, uncleanness into purity, sinfulness
> into holiness, creature into Creator, human into
> God! A marvelous work!
>
> LOUIS DE MONTFORT, *The Secret of Mary*

Mother of a Thousand Faces

After many years I asked Sisters Rosemarie and Jo-Ann how I might repay their kindness to me. They asked me to produce a contemporary version of one of their founding texts, *The Love of Eternal Wisdom* by Father Louis de Montfort. My translation was a hit among the Daughters of Wisdom worldwide, and they sent me to Rome to teach their leadership team.

My thesis was that Mary is one of many faces of the Divine Mother. While the sisters in Rome heard the same wisdom in all of Mother's incarnations, they could not take that final step with me and believe it was the same voice speaking through each incarnation.

God speaks in only one voice.

People are taught to hear only echoes.

The idea of the supernatural as being something over and above the natural is a killing idea. . . . This is one of the glorious things about the mother-goddess religions, where the world is the body of the Goddess, divine in itself, and divinity isn't something ruling over and above a fallen nature.

JOSEPH CAMPBELL, *The Power of Myth*

Kali Das

Swami Atmarupananda was my Hindu teacher during our ten-year tenure at Ed Bastian's Spiritual Paths Institute. Swami-ji was a member of the Ramakrishna Order of Vedanta Hinduism. It was under his guidance that in 2010 I received initiation in the Ramakrishna Order under his teacher, Swami Swahananda.

The ceremony was simple, though exhausting for Swami Swahananda, who was in the closing months of his life. He asked me to place flowers and fruit on the altar, and he taught me a mantra I was to repeat daily and never share privately or

publically. He explained
that this mantra was
chosen to deepen my
experiences with and
love for the Mother.

I had neglected to ask Swami for a "Hindu name,"
but a few years later I had a dream in which Mother Kali came
and called me Kali Das, "Servant of Kali." I had the name
"verified" by several swamis, and while I don't use the name, I
value it as a sign of holy rascality. To be in service to Kali, the
destroyer of delusions, is a humbling honor.

At last I was one of the Das brothers, sharing a last name
with my teachers Ram Dass, Surya Das, and Krishna Das.

He's a Holy Rascal

As I mentioned in my interview with AltGuru in chapter 2,
the title *holy rascal* came from Jose Hobday, a Franciscan nun
and Seneca elder. I was lecturing at the Aspen Chapel as part
of an event organized by the Spiritual Paths Institute. When I
finished speaking, Sister Jose, who had been sitting in the very
back row, pulled herself up and shouted gleefully, "He's a holy
rascal!" She should know.

Years earlier Sister Jose was invited to meet the Dalai Lama.
She was told to offer His Holiness a *khata*, a white ceremonial
scarf that he would take from her and place around her neck.
At no point was she to make any physical contact with His
Holiness. As the Dalai Lama bent down to place the khata
around her neck, Sister Jose reached up, pinched his cheeks,
and shook his face, saying, "I can do this to you. You're my
baby brother!" His Holiness laughed. His lamas gasped.

That's a holy rascal.

I like flying kites because it is such a wild, freeing thing. I think God works within lifted spirits. That is true, I think, of any kind of play—running, roller skating, rolling in the leaves, just kicking around and making noise, wasting time, having a party. I still believe God is present in those playful moments, just as my mother taught me.

SISTER JOSE HOBDAY,
Stories of Awe and Abundance

Religion
UNVEILED
The Tao of Toto

Pay no attention to that
man behind the curtain.
The Wizard of Oz

4
Religion and Language

Religions are like languages: all languages are of human origin; each language reflects and shapes the civilization that speaks it; all languages make meaning out of the raw facts of our existence; no language is true or false; there are things you can say in one language that you cannot say (or say as well) in another; the more languages you know, the more nuanced your understanding of life becomes; and as important as languages are, the final "language" of wisdom is silence.

Substitute the word *religion* for *language*, and you have the basic holy rascal understanding of religion.

> We turn sounds into letters, letters into words, words into sentences, sentences into paragraphs, paragraphs into books, books into excuses for bashing one another's heads in. No wonder silence is golden.   RR

5
Religions—Healthy and Unhealthy

Religions aren't "true" or "false," but rather "healthy" or "unhealthy." Healthy religions are about universal wisdom and love, about providing meaning in a way that opens your heart, sharpens your mind, and unclenches your fists. Healthy religion invites you to meet those of other religions and ask, "What can I learn from you?" rather than, "How can I get you to think like me?"

Unhealthy religions are about power and control, imposing meaning in a manner that inhibits questioning, doubt, or learning from those labeled as "other." Unhealthy religions worship conformity: are you towing the line, staying true to tradition, upholding ancient opinions in the name of sacred truths?

Healthy religions have porous boundaries, welcoming the truth wherever it is found. Unhealthy religions have rigid boundaries and obsess over who is in and who is out, who can marry whom, and who can pee where.

A religion is often healthy and unhealthy at the same time.

Evil, when we are in its power, is not felt as evil, but as a necessity, even a duty.

Simone Weil, *Gravity and Grace*

6

Religiosity and Religion

Religiosity is the innate, ancient, and ongoing human capacity for meaning making. Religion is the result of meaning making reflecting specific times, tribes, and mores. Religiosity is rooted in curiosity about what is so. Religion is rooted in belief about what we are told is so. Religiosity is about engaging the present. Religion is about preserving the past. Religiosity has no fixed content and remains open to truth even as our understanding of truth evolves. Religion has prescribed content and clings to old truths even when they are shown to be false. Religiosity has teachers who point beyond themselves. Religion has leaders who point only toward themselves. Religiosity wants you to be awake. Religion prefers you to be asleep.

The true enemies of one religion aren't those of another religion, or even those with no religion, but those within the religion who use it for their own ends. **RR**

7
Saints and Scoundrels

Saints place their religion in service to religiosity. Scoundrels place their religion in service to themselves. Saints interpret their texts and traditions to promote compassion and justice. Scoundrels interpret their texts and traditions to promote fear, hatred, violence, and their own power. Saints want to set you free. Scoundrels want to enslave you.

Don't imagine it's easy to tell the saint from the scoundrel. Saints can masquerade as scoundrels. Scoundrels always masquerade as saints. But the real problem isn't who's dressing up as whom, but rather your tendency to follow the one who tells you what you want to hear—and that is more often than not the scoundrel.

> Saints and scoundrels both claim to know something you don't. Saints want to teach so you too will know. Scoundrels want to be worshiped so you never have to know. RR

8
Few Want to Be Free

Few people want to be free. Few people want to think for themselves. Few people want to live life without the (faux) safety net of creeds, traditions, and beliefs. Most of us prefer to follow a leader, repeat hallowed (and often hollow) thoughts, and adhere to the tried and true even when it proves to be tired and false. This isn't a criticism, but merely an observation. Freedom is difficult, thinking is challenging, living without a net is frightening; so it shouldn't be surprising that most people prefer the easier path of brand-name religion.

What is surprising and should be surprising is that so many people know they are doing this. People aren't stupid, but we are lazy.

A religious mind demands diligence to be precise, to be accurate, objectively and inwardly, so that there is no illusion, no deception, total integrity. That is what can be called a mind that is religious. But religion as it exists is not religion at all. All the propaganda, the images in the West, and the images in the East, you know, the whole rituals, the whole dressing up and all that business, has nothing whatsoever to do with religion.

J. KRISHNAMURTI[5]

9

First There Is Religion, Then There Is No Religion, Then There Is

There's no such thing as Hinduism, Judaism, Buddhism, Christianity, or Islam. There are only Hinduisms, Judaisms, Buddhisms, Christianities, and Islams. Orthodox and Reform Judaisms, for example, aren't two denominations of a single faith, they are two very different faiths, two very different Judaisms: the first subsuming the individual to tradition, the second subsuming tradition to the individual. While each claims the mantle of Moses, neither admits that the Moses to whom it lays claim is a figment of its own imagination.

The same can be said of every religion.

When one Muslim claims Islam is a religion of peace and another says Islam is a religion of war, both are wrong and both are right. The Islam of the peaceful Muslim is a religion of peace. The Islam of the violent Muslim is an Islam of war. It isn't that one is real and the other false, but that there is no real Islam at all.   RR

10.
Religions Are Made Up

Religions are made up. This isn't a bad thing: everything we humans do is made up. Religions are made up the same way Beethoven's Ninth Symphony is made up, and the same way Margaret Fuller's Transcendentalism is made up, and the same way Freud's psychotherapy is made up. This is what it is to be human: we make things up.

Some of what we make up is liberating, and some of what we make up is enslaving; some of what we make up is utopian, and some of what we make up is dystopian; some of what we make up can be proven by science, and some of what we make up can be proven by poetry; but it is all made up.

The problem isn't that religion is made up; the problem is that religions can't admit they are made up.
RR

11
Branded by the Light

The goal of every religion is to become a brand: a product that captures people's imaginations, engages their emotions, triggers their passions, and earns their loyalty by promising to fulfill the desires the brand itself instills within them. A brand is a self-fulfilling prophecy that rests solely in the mind of the loyalist, the believer. But when a religion becomes a brand, it becomes a prisoner of the brand. It can't change because even when its leaders want to change, its customers won't let it change. Remember New Coke?

For a religion to change in the present it must first rewrite its past so that no change is necessary.

RR

12

Endless Curiosity and Boundless Compassion

There are two essential qualities to holy rascality: endless curiosity and boundless compassion. We are endlessly curious regarding what people believe and have boundless compassion for the people who believe it.

We know the power of belief to capture our imagination and shape our behavior. We know that all of us can become trapped in unhealthy religions and fall prey to charismatic clerics whose private lust for power is masked beneath public piety. And we know that to violently tear down a faith can be as damaging as letting things be. Our way is not the way of hate proclaiming all religion is evil; our way is the way of humor pointing out the absurdities to which all religions are prone.

> Yertle the Turtle was toppled by Mack, the turtle at the very bottom of Yertle's towering turtle hierarchy. Mack burped, and the tower fell. Today burping isn't enough. Today Mack must laugh and get us laughing with him, until the joy of laughter overcomes the fear of faithful.   RR

13
Snake or Belt?

Here is a version of a marvelous Hindu parable that speaks to the heart of holy rascality: Imagine you awaken in the middle of the night to find a poisonous snake curled up next to your leg on your bed. Afraid to move or speak lest you startle the snake into striking your leg, you spend the night frozen in terror. As the room lightens with the coming of dawn, you discover the "snake" is merely a coiled belt you neglected to put away the night before. The terror instantly disappears, and you laugh at your own foolishness.

Holy rascals help people laugh at their foolishness by first learning to laugh at their own. Holy rascals don't ridicule the "snake," only help us to see the belt.

All religions promise a reward for excellences of the will or heart, but none for the excellences of the head or understanding.

Arthur Schopenhauer,
The World as Will and Representation

14
Our Motto, Our Guide, Our Mantra, Our Goal

Our motto is the Sanskrit *neti neti*—"not this, not that." Truth can't be packaged into any religion, -ism, or ideology. Truth is simply reality as it is in this and every moment. A packaged truth is at least once removed from the actual Truth.

Our guide is Lao Tzu, the sixth-century Chinese poet, who wrote, "The tao that can be named is not the eternal Tao" (*Tao Te Ching* 1:1). The God that can be branded is not the eternal God. The religion that can be packaged is not the eternal religion. The theology that can be imagined is not the eternal theology.

Our mantra is the Kalama Sutra: "Believe nothing because a wise person said it. Believe nothing because it is generally held. Believe nothing because it is written. Believe nothing because it is said to be Divine. Believe nothing because others believe it. Believe only what you yourself judge to be true."

In a world that really has been turned on its head, truth is a moment of falsehood.
Guy Debord, *The Society of the Spectacle*

And then question even that.

Our goal is to be "a blessing to all the families of the earth" (Genesis 12:3) by helping you know yourself and all beings as manifestings of God (however named).

15
No Clinging

Holy rascals follow the advice of Seng-Ts'an (529–609 AD),
the Third Patriarch of Ch'an Buddhism: "Seek not after
Truth; cease only to cling to opinions" (*Hsin-Hsin Ming*).
It isn't that we have no opinions; it's that we don't cling
to them. Holy rascals are never certain. Always living
with uncertainty, we pull the rug of surety out from under
our own feet before we help pull it out from under the
feet of others.

There are two traps into which holy rascals fall:
we forget to be holy, or we forget to be rascals.
Forgetting to be holy, we are mean. Forgetting
to be rascals, we are meaningless.   RR

16
One Aim

Holy rascals have only one aim: to pull the curtain back on parochial religion in order to liberate people from the Great and Terrible Wizards who use religion to frighten them into submission and to manipulate them into doing evil under the banner of good.

We are not antireligion; we are anti–unhealthy religion: religion that promotes a world of "us against them" and sanctions the exploitation, oppression, and even murder of "them" in this world and the torture of "them" in the next.

We are not antibelief; we are anti–irrational belief: belief that substitutes ancient fiction for modern science.

We are not anti-God; we are anti–mad Gods: Gods who sanction the lust for power that fuels those who invented them.

Holy rascals don't yearn for the end of Hinduism, Judaism, Buddhism, Christianity, Islam, and the rest; we yearn for their liberation from the foolishness of Hindus, Jews, Buddhists, Christians, and Muslims.

> There is no need for temple or church, for mosque or synagogue, no need for complicated philosophy, doctrine, or dogma. Our own heart, our own mind, is the temple. The doctrine is compassion.
>
> HIS HOLINESS THE DALAI LAMA,
> *Ethics for the New Millennium*

17

Truth Is What's Common to All

Religiosity is the art of making meaning through story, symbol, ritual, and prayer. The tools of religiosity are, as the Zen people say, fingers pointing toward the moon, and they should not be mistaken for the moon itself. Healthy religions know this and use their tools to point beyond themselves. Unhealthy religions reject this, insisting that the tool is the Truth rather than a pointer to the Truth. Healthy religions ascribe to the teaching "Truth is one. Different people call it by different names" (*Rig-Veda* 1.164.46). Unhealthy religions ascribe to a slightly different teaching: "Truth is one. And we own it."

For the present age, which prefers the sign to the thing signified, the copy to the original, representation to reality, the appearance to the essence . . . illusion only is sacred, truth profane. Nay, sacredness is held to be enhanced in proportion as truth decreases and illusion increases, so that the highest degree of illusion comes to be the highest degree of sacredness.

LUDWIG FEUERBACH, *The Essence of Christianity*

18
Piety and Homicide

When religions use their stories, symbols, rituals, and prayers to point toward the Truth, they draw attention away from themselves and toward the Truth. When religions insist their stories, symbols, rituals, and prayers are the Truth, they draw attention away from the Truth and toward themselves.

When a religion is mistaken for the Truth, other religions are mistaken for the enemy of the Truth.

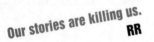

When a religion claims a monopoly on Truth, it often elevates homicide to an act of piety. For example, when Yahweh saw that the Israelites were intermarrying with the Moabites and bringing Brand X, the religion of Baal, into the shelf space reserved for Brand Y(ahweh), he ordered the Israelite leadership impaled (Numbers 25:4).

When you see evil done in the name of a religion, don't imagine this is a perversion of an otherwise peaceful and loving religion. Rather know that it is a perverse reading of that religion vying with other readings of that religion for control of the brand.

19

What Is Exclusive Is Not True; What Is True Is Not Exclusive

Exclusivist claims are marketing slogans: Coke is "the Real Thing," the United States is "Number One," BMW is "the Ultimate Driving Machine." What is true of these brands is true of brand-name religions as well: Christians claim, "There is no salvation outside the Church," the Jews are "God's Chosen People," the Qur'an is the uncorrupted "Word of God," the Buddha is the "Awakened One," et cetera. Religions make such claims in order to stand out from the competition. But Truth is not exclusive to any religion. On the contrary, Truth is true for all, or it isn't Truth.

At the mystic heart of every religion are the four points of Perennial Wisdom: (1) all beings are manifestings of the singular Reality we call God, Brahman, Allah, Nature, Universe, Dharmakaya, et cetera; (2) we humans have an innate capacity to know ourselves and all life as a manifesting of Reality; (3) knowing this gives rise to an ethic of universal compassion and justice; and (4) knowing this and living this ethic is the highest calling of every human being.

> The best ideas are common property.
> Lucius Annaeus Seneca[6]

Holy rascals pull the rug out from the exclusivist claims of every religion in order to reveal the Perennial Wisdom at the heart of all religions.

20.
All Is God

Perennial Wisdom's
understanding of
God—the Absolute, Allah,
Kali, Yahweh, Mother, the
Trinity, Brahman, Krishna,
Spirit, Nature, Reality, et

If God is infinite, God is everything. If you say, "This is God but that is not," your God is too small, yet not so small as to do no harm.
RR

cetera—is panentheistic: the understanding that all (*pan*)
reality is in (*en*) God (*theos*) as a part of God and that God
is greater than the sum of its parts. Panentheism differs from
pantheism in that the latter doesn't posit this "greater than."

Here are three expressions of panentheism:

> God is found in all things and all things are found
> in God. . . .
>
> Everything is in God, and God is in everything
> and beyond everything, and there is nothing other
> than God.
>
> **RABBI MOSHE CORDOVERO**, Sefer Elimah (Daf 24b)

> All reality is pervaded by Me, yet my form is not
> seen. All living things have their being in Me, yet
> I am not limited by them.
>
> **BHAGAVAD GITA 9:4**

> God is that in whom we live and move and have
> our being.
>
> **ACTS 17:28**

21
You Can Know God Directly

Because God is everything, everything you encounter is God.

While you may appreciate one belief system over another, while you may prefer chanting to praying and participating in one set of rituals rather than another, know that none of them are necessary to knowing God. You know God because you are God.

Of course anyone can claim to know God and to be God, and many do. How can we judge the authenticity of their claim? First, those who know God as All never claim to be all of God. While it is true that the ocean is the entirety of every wave, it is not true that any wave is the entirety of the ocean.

Second, those who know God as All aren't selling anything. While they may belong to and cherish a religion, they aren't telling you to join that religion.

Third, those who know God as All don't tell you what to believe; they only invite you to see what is and to know what you already know if you only give yourself permission to know it.

Life is too short to be someone you don't want to be. If life were taller, things might be different, but it isn't, so they're not.

RR

22
Knowing God, Acting Godly

According to the philosopher and religious thinker Martin Buber (1878–1965), there are two ways to encounter life: *I–It* and *I–Thou*. An I–It encounter treats the one you encounter as a means: an object to be used for your own benefit. An I–Thou encounter treats the one you encounter as an end: a unique and precious manifesting of the One deserving of your utmost respect. This is true whether you are encountering a fellow human, an animal, a tree, or any other manifesting of the Divine: "Every means is an obstacle. Only where all means have disintegrated can encounters occur."[7]

Knowing God is not at the expense of knowing the other. Knowing God is knowing the other as a manifesting of God. And with this knowing one naturally treats the other well.

> If people's beliefs—secular or religious—make them belligerent, intolerant, and unkind . . . they are not "skillful." If, however, their convictions impel them to act compassionately and to honor the stranger, then they are good, helpful, and sound. This is the test of true religiosity.
>
> KAREN ARMSTRONG, *The Great Transformation*

23
This Is Why You Are Here

Some claim that life is a test or a school. But for the holy rascal, life is a playground. You aren't here to earn your way into heaven or to graduate to a higher grade or better incarnation. You are here to play, and the game you are here to play is called Wake Up!

Wake up to the nonduality of God permeating and transcending the duality of self and other. Wake up to the interdependence of good and evil, up and down, in and out, self and other, I and Thou. Wake up to your insatiable appetite for self-destruction. Wake up to your inexhaustible capacity for Self-realization. Wake up to the ways you fall prey to fearsome and fear-filled religions. Wake up to the Perennial Wisdom imprinted on your heart. Wake up to the madness that passes for Reality. Wake up to the Reality that surpasses all madness. Wake up from magical thinking that reduces God and the universe to your cosmic concierge. Wake up to the real magic of alchemy: transforming the lead of egoism into the gold of Self, knowing all the while that ego and Self are both God.

> Perennial Wisdom is the Whac-A-Mole of human religiosity: hammered by the parochial and yet popping up over and again to the frustration of those who fear Truth.
>
> RR

24
God Doesn't Exist; God Is Existing

If holy rascals have a theology—and many don't—it is this: God is greater than but never other than the manifesting universe. God is the Greater Happening happening as the universe.

Look closely enough, and every "thing" dissolves into happening. Look even closer, and every happening dissolves into Happening. This Happening is God. Jews call this happening YHVH, from the Hebrew verb meaning "to be." God is a verb, and so-called things are in fact gerunds.

One of the major fallacies to which we humans are prone is the concept of things. A thing is inanimate, static, fixed. But there is nothing in the universe that fits that description. Indeed, there is no "thing" in the universe at all. If evolution teaches us anything (assuming you live in a place where evolution itself can be taught), it's that the universe is alive, fluid, and forever surprising itself.

Why is there something rather than nothing? Because you aren't looking deeply enough.

RR

25
Maya

Evolution pulls the curtain back on so-called things to reveal happenings. The universe is *tohu va vohu* (Genesis 1:2): a wild, chaotic symphony of happenings that every once in a while bursts into Beethoven's "Ode to Joy" or Leonard Cohen's "Hallelujah" or Carol King's "Will You Still Love Me Tomorrow" or Anoushka Shankar's "Rise." And yet we are addicted to the illusion of things and impose nouns where there are only gerunds. This addiction gives a false impression of what reality is. This false impression is what we call *maya*.

> Spirituality is the art of disentangling ourselves from the stories that condition us in order to engage directly with the unmediated manifestings of God.
>
> **RR**

Maya is the defining characteristic of our world view when our world view is rooted in the illusion of things and nouns. When we say, "It is raining," we invent an "it" that rains, but there is no "it" or even "rain;" there is only "raining." We live in an illusory world of grammatical ghosts distracting us from the reality of happenings. When we live in a world of ghosts, we imagine God as the Supreme Ghost, the It of its and Noun of nouns, and so fail to know God as God is: the Happening that is happening as all happening.

26
God Is Dead; Long Live God*ing*

The great task of the holy rascal is to free the mind from nouns and for gerunds. One way we do this is to be the child who admits the obvious, the emperor has no clothes, and in so doing to de*NOUN*ce God, to de-thing the Holy It, and to defang the religions that support It.

God isn't a thing or a being or even the Supreme Being. God is *being* itself. God is the Happening that is happening as all happening. God is process. God is God*ing*. God isn't the river (as Heraclitus taught us, even the river isn't the river!) but the flowing. The happening we call "river" is in fact God*ing* river*ing*.

There are no nouns, only gerunds: only God*ing*, tree*ing*, elephant*ing*, woman*ing*, man*ing*, natur*ing*, you*ing*, and I*ing*.

> When playing with religious ideas, rituals, and symbols, our goal is to reclaim the immediacy of the event toward which they point. No more secondhand God. RR

27
The Ice Cream That Cannot Be Flavored

Walk into an ice cream shop and order a scoop of ice cream. The clerk will ask which flavor of ice cream you prefer, but you don't want a flavor, you want ice cream. The clerk is stymied. Of all the flavors on the menu, "ice cream" isn't one of them. You can order chocolate, vanilla, strawberry, or rum raisin, but you can't order ice cream. It is the same with God.

Walk into any temple, synagogue, church, or mosque and ask for God, and you will be introduced to the flavor of God that that temple, synagogue, church, or mosque sells. When you explain that you aren't interested in a flavor of God, but rather God alone, the cleric will be stymied.

Einstein was right: God doesn't play dice with the universe. God plays mah-jongg. On Wednesdays. With Mrs. Friedman and her neighbors.

RR

No House of God offers you God, only flavors of God: YHVH, Allah, the Trinity, the Mother, Brahman, Dharmakaya, Spirit, and dozens of others—but you cannot have just God.

What the holy rascal wants is just God. Just God comes with no label, no organization, no hierarchy, no theology, no book, no magic, and no promise. Just God doesn't take sides, choose peoples, save some, and damn others. Just God is simply the Happening happening as all happening.

28
Brand-Name Gods

Brand-name Gods are products of our imagination, desiring what we desire, despising what we despise, and sanctioning our lust for power while condemning that same lust in our enemies:

YHVH commands genocide against the Seven Nations of Canaan (Deuteronomy 7) because the Israelites wanted to occupy their land.

Allah commands Muslims to "kill the unbeliever wherever you find them" (Qur'an 2:191) because the Muslims wanted to remove the competition.

Krishna tells Arjuna, "If you kill without attachment, regardless how many you kill, your action carries no evil" (Bhagavad Gita 18:17) because the Pandavas kings wanted to eliminate their Kauravas rivals.

God eternally damns "those who did not know God and those who did not obey the gospel of our Lord Jesus" (2 Thessalonians 1:5–9) because the apostle Paul wanted to keep his Christians in line.

Brand-name Gods are always in the service to those who hold the brand's copyright.

When once a certain class of people has been placed by the temporal and spiritual authorities outside the ranks of those whose life has value, then nothing comes more naturally to men than murder.

SIMONE WEIL, *Selected Essays, 1934–1943*

29
Without God All Things Are Permitted

In Fyodor Dostoyevsky's novel *The Brothers Karamazov*, Ivan argues that without God all manner of evil would be permitted. The opposite is no less true.

Inspired by YHVH, the prophet Elijah ordered the slaughter of the priests of Baal (1 Kings 18:40). The people who did the slaughtering thought God was good and assumed that their actions were also good because God commanded them. The people being slaughtered thought this same God was evil and what was being done to them was evil. With God all things are permitted!

When Muslims speak of Allah as *al-Rahman al-Rahim*, All Merciful, All Compassionate, they think Allah is good. When ISIS beheads people in the name of Allah, they too think that Allah is good and that beheading is good. But the beheaded think Allah is evil (or they did until there were beheaded, at which point they stopped thinking altogether). God is only as good as the deeds of believers.

With great power comes great responsibility. With absolute power comes none.
RR

What is good is what benefits the well-being of all beings. What is evil is what benefits the well-being of some at the expense of others. If your God is biased, your God isn't God, only an excuse for doing what you want.

30.

The Greatest Fundraising Gimmick of All Time

The good that God demands is always good for those
who insist God demands it. The question holy rascals
ask isn't "Is God Good?" but "Cui bono: who benefits
from the 'goodness' of God?" Take, for example, this
story from the New Testament:

Ananias and his
wife Sapphira sold
some property, and
after putting a
percentage of the
proceeds aside
for themselves,
Ananias brought the rest
to Peter as a donation to the church. Peter
asked Ananias if this was all the money earned from the
sale. Ananias claimed it was. "You have lied to God!" Peter
screamed, and Ananias instantly "collapsed and died."

*Who benefits most from God isn't
the believer, but those who craft the
beliefs in which the believer believes.*

RR

Three hours later Peter asked Sapphira, who knew
nothing of her husband's death, if she and Ananias had
turned over all the monies from the sale of their property.
When she said they had, Peter told her what had happened
to her husband, adding, "The very men who buried your
husband are now here to bury you!" Then Sapphira, too,
fell to the floor and died. "And a great fear seized the entire
church . . ." (Acts 5:1–11).

Who benefits from this story? Only Peter.

31
Father Knows Best

Brand-name Gods are in service to the elites who invent them. Therefore, don't merely do what God says, investigate who benefits from God saying it.

One of the most frightening theological ideas is Søren Kierkegaard's "the teleological suspension of the ethical." The idea is simple: God is good and would never ask you do something bad, even if it looks bad to you, so do what God says regardless of what you think about it. In other words: trust God and abandon your capacity to think critically and act morally.

We must question the story logic of having an all-knowing all-powerful God, who creates faulty humans, and then blames them for his own mistakes.
Gene Roddenberry[8]

The problem with this is just as simple: The God you're trusting is a brand-name God imagined by an elite for the benefit of that elite. To trust this God is to surrender yourself to this elite. For example:

> You are obligated to fight even though doing so is hateful to you. But consider this: perhaps you mistakenly hate something that is good for you, or perhaps you mistakenly desire something that is bad for you. Only Allah knows what is good and bad, you do not (Qur'an 2:216).

32
Free Will

Even when we ask why God allows evil, we excuse God from being evil by taking refuge in the notion of free will. God gave us free will, and we use our free will to do evil. Evil isn't God's fault; it's our fault. But why did God give us free will?

Why couldn't God have created us without free will? What would we lose if we were incapable of doing evil—if we lacked the capacity for hatred, racism, anti-Semitism, sexism, homophobia, ecocide, homicide, and the rest? And if we were created without free will, would we even know it?

If you lacked the ability to do evil, would you complain, "I wish I had free will so I could rape and pillage and plunder and murder"? The thought would never cross your mind because the very idea of evil would be unimaginable.

The reason we are taught God gave us free will and therefore the capacity to do evil is that without this belief, we cannot reward those who do what we like and condemn those who don't. Without free will, heaven and hell (or a better or worse rebirth) make no sense.

Here's the thing about free will.
It isn't free.

RR

33
God's Ultimate Escape Hatch

Knowing how free will is used to excuse God from the charge of being evil doesn't mean there is no such thing as free will. There might be, but we can't know for certain one way or the other. It doesn't mean people are puppets. We might be, but, again, there is no way to know this for certain.

We aren't making some huge philosophical affirmation: THERE IS NO SUCH THING AS FREE WILL. We are only saying that whether or not free will exists, we use the idea of free will to excuse God from having to take responsibility for the quality of life by blaming people and the way we choose to live our lives.

> If I could do anything I want, I would first have to know what it is I want and not what I am conditioned to want by religion, politics, and ad agencies. And that may be fundamentally unknowable.   RR

34
Functional Free Will

We certainly have a sense of free will or what we might call *functional free will*. We still have the sense of choice even if conditioning, genes, or genies condition the choices we make. We still have to choose even if our choices are preset.

> Humans can do what they will, but they cannot will what they will.
> Arthur Schopenhauer,
> *Essays and Aphorisms*

Imagine you and a friend jump off a cliff to your deaths. You believe in free will and insist to your friend as you fall that you both chose to die. Your friend believes all actions are predetermined and says you were both fated to die.

To paraphrase Bashō: High cliff—fools jump off—splat!

The truth is, no matter what story you tell yourself, you are fated to choose. And that is all the free will you need.

35
We've Got the Power

Gods claim to be all-powerful. They're not.

If Krishna were all-powerful, Hindus wouldn't eat beef. If YHVH were all-powerful, Jews wouldn't eat pork. If Jesus were all-powerful, Catholics wouldn't use condoms, and Southern Baptists wouldn't have abortions. If Allah were all-powerful, Muslims wouldn't drink alcohol. Yet Hindus do eat beef, Jews do eat pork, Catholics do use condoms, Southern Baptists do have abortions, and Muslims do drink alcohol—not all, of course, but some. Indeed, if only one violated the laws of her God, she would prove the limitations of her God's power. It isn't that your God lets you violate his laws; it is that he can't stop you from doing so. Why? Because your God doesn't exist. Your God is a figment of the imagination of people who have issues with beef, pork, condoms, abortions, or alcohol and who, with some very bloody and violent exceptions, lack the capacity to force people to live according to their issues.

God is a comfort: commanding us to do what we want, forgiving us for doing what others don't want, and promising to reward us for both.

RR

36
God, the Eternal I

Regardless of the name we use—YHVH, Allah, Christ, Mother, the Trinity, Krishna, Vishnu, Shiva, Kali, Quetzalcoatl, Ahura Mazda, or the rest—when we talk about God, we make God an object. Even the Perennial Wisdom notion that God is the Happening happening as all happening at this moment perpetuates God as object. But there are no objects, no things, no its, and insisting otherwise is the stuff of maya. The truest name of God, the only name that doesn't make God into an it, is "I."

I am the Alpha and the Omega. The First and the Last. The Beginning and the End (Jesus Christ, in Revelation 22:13).

I am the First and the Last. Apart from me there is nothing else (YHVH, in Isaiah 44:6).

I am the Truth (Mansur Al-Hallaj).

I am the One, the Many, the All-pervading, the All-encompassing (Krishna, in the Bhagavad Gita 9:13).

Tell them I sent you (Exodus 3:14).

When we look into God's eyes, we say, "Thou." When we look through God's eyes, we say only, "I."

This pure I AM state is not hard to achieve and impossible to escape. . . . You can never run from Spirit, because Spirit is the runner. . . . Why on earth do you keep looking for God when God is actually the looker?

KEN WILBER, *The Simple Feeling of Being*

37
Liar, Lunatic, or Lord?

The Christian apologist C. S. Lewis put this question to his audience: "When Jesus says, 'I am the Way, the Truth, and the Life. No one comes to the Father except through me' (John 14:6), is he a liar, a lunatic, or the Lord?" The question is called Lewis's trilemma.

Lewis couldn't imagine anyone choosing "liar" or "lunatic" and hence assumed his trilemma was a surefire evangelical trap: when forced to choose, the chooser could only choose "Lord" and would convert to Christianity on the spot. Yet imagine placing a similar trilemma before Mr. Lewis himself:

When **Muhammad** (PBUH) claimed to have received the Holy Qur'an from Allah through the archangel Gabriel, was he a liar, a lunatic, or the Prophet of God?

When **Joseph Smith** claimed that God charged him with founding the one true Christian Church, the Church of Jesus Christ of Latter-Day Saints, was he a liar, a lunatic, or the Prophet of God?

When **Krishna** claimed "all reality is My being, and yet I am greater still" (Bhagavad Gita 9:4), was he a liar, a lunatic, or the Lord?

The trilemma is simply an example of confirmation bias.

A holy rascal response to Lewis's trilemma: "We are liars when we claim we aren't God, lunatics when we imagine we are all of God, and Lord when we know God is all of us."

38
Confirmation Bias

I have no doubt Mr. Lewis would choose "liar" or "lunatic" in the case of Muhammad, Smith, and Krishna; so why not in the case of Jesus? The answer is simple: Mr. Lewis already believes Jesus is Lord. Lewis's trilemma is an example of confirmation bias: the unconscious tendency to assume what you believe to be true is in fact true and to then interpret all situations in light of that truth.

> Jesus wasn't a liar, a lunatic, or the Lord. He was a mystic, a poet, and a wisdom sage.
>
> **RR**

From Lewis's point of view, his trilemma is simply a trap set to catch nonbelievers in the politically incorrect act of calling the God of 2.2 billion Christians a charlatan or madman.

The fact that 2.2 billion Christians believe God had a son doesn't mean the 4 billion Hindus, Jews, Muslims, and Buddhists who do not believe this are wrong. It only means that 2.2 billion Christians who do believe God had a son cannot believe the 4 billion who don't believe this are right.

39
No Gap

God is the infinite, all-pervading and all-encompassing Happening happening as all happening. There can be no gap between you and God, between *atman* (soul) and Brahman, between your "I" and Ehyeh, the I'*ing* of all being. There is only what the Buddhists call *Tathātā*: "suchness," "what is so," "the nature of things," reality.

When Jesus says, "Before Abraham was, I am" (John 8:57) and "I am the Way, the Truth, and the Life. No one comes to the Father except through me" (John 14:6), he isn't speaking as a thirtysomething Jew from Nazareth, but as the cosmic Christ; not the "I" that imagines itself apart from God, but the I'*ing* that is God (Exodus 3:14); not the alienated self, but the Self that knows itself as all selves: the atman who is Brahman.

Like Jesus's interlocutors who cannot imagine how this young man can be older than Abraham, C. S. Lewis is deaf to the deeper meaning of the Gospel and imagines a flat Jesus who can only be liar, lunatic, or Lord rather than a fully God-realized Jesus who knows that "I and the Father are one, and so are you."

A person who imagines herself separate from God imagines herself greater than God, for she points to her skin and says to God, "You may come this far, and no further." RR

40

Et Tu, Krishna?

Lord Krishna says,

> I am the Self, seated in the hearts of all beings; I am
> the beginning of all, and I am the end of all. I am
> nature; I am the Mind; I am the Intelligence in all
> that lives. I am Life (Bhagavad Gita 10:20, 22–23).

Like Jesus's "I," Krishna's "I" is the fully God-realized "I." This
"I" is you. And although you are not all of "I," "I" is all of you.

Krishna knew this and said, "I am the Life"; Jesus knew this
and said, "I am the Way, the Truth, and the Life"; Al-Mansur
knew this and said, "I am Truth"; Abraham Abulafia knew this
and said, "God is I, and I am God."

Understand this, and you understand the only Truth
you need.

The universe is God's
unauthorized autobiography.
RR

41
Sacred Dis-Ease

Every brand-name religion says there is something wrong with you. For Hinduism it's ignorance, for Judaism it's exile, for Buddhism it's craving, for Christianity it's sin, and for Islam it's pride. When you are born into or choose a religion, you inherit that religion's particular dis-ease: the existential trauma that religion is uniquely designed to cure.

When your religion diagnoses you with a certain dis-ease, always get a second opinion. Preferably from a different religion.

RR

The dis-ease is central to the religion's story. If there were nothing wrong with you, you'd have no need for a religion. Or if what was wrong with you wasn't what the religion could cure, you'd have no need for that religion.

For example, if you're baptized into the Catholic faith, congratulations! You now suffer from the dis-ease of Original Sin. If, on the other hand, you choose to be a Jew, mazel tov! No Original Sin; Jews never heard of it. Yet if you are a Jew and you believe you suffer from Catholicism's Original Sin, Judaism is the wrong medicine, and you need to convert to Catholicism in order to be cured.

The first thing a religion does is convince you there is something wrong. The second thing is to convince you it can set things right.

42
Religious Dis-Eases Are Iatrogenic

The word *iatrogenic* comes from the Greek: *iatros*, meaning "doctor or healer," and *gennen*, meaning "as a result of." A physical, mental, or emotional problem is iatrogenic if caused by a doctor.

The difference between something that is medically iatrogenic and something that is religiously iatrogenic is that the former is inadvertent, while the latter is deliberate. Hinduism makes ignorance a dis-ease, Judaism makes exile a dis-ease, Buddhism makes craving a dis-ease, Christianity makes sin a dis-ease, and Islam makes pride a dis-ease. And they do so in order to then offer you the cure to the dis-ease they created.

The mystery of life isn't a problem to be solved, but a reality to experience.
Frank Herbert, *Dune*

43
Religion as Munchausen Syndrome

Munchausen syndrome is a mental disorder in which you pretend to be ill in order to gain attention and sympathy. Munchausen syndrome is named for Baron von Munchausen (1720–1797), an officer in the German army famous for spinning outrageous yarns about his wartime exploits.

Munchausen syndrome is called a *factitious disorder*, meaning it has no basis in fact.

The difference between religion and snake oil is that snake oil promises to cure a real disease while religion promises to cure an imaginary one.

RR

The dis-eases of brand-name religions are the same. Sticking with our Original Sin example: Billions of people alive today suffer from Original Sin stemming from Eve and Adam's eating the forbidden fruit of the Tree of Knowledge of Good and Evil. But to suffer from Original Sin, you must first believe that this story is history, and that through Adam sin entered the world (Romans 5:12), and that because of Adam we are all "slaves to sin" until "set free" by Jesus Christ (Romans 6:20, 22). But what if the Garden of Eden story is just that—a story rather than a diagnosis of a dis-ease?

Without mistaking story for history, the dis-ease of Original Sin disappears, and with it the need for Jesus to die as ransom for our sins (1 Timothy 2:6).

44

TEACH YOUR CHILDREN WELL
Religion as Munchausen Syndrome by Proxy

Claiming you suffer from a disease you do not have in order to gain sympathy and attention from others is Munchausen syndrome. Insisting your children suffer from a disease they do not have in order to gain for yourself the sympathy and attention of others is Munchausen syndrome by proxy. Believing in one brand-name religion or another is a form of Munchausen syndrome; raising your children to believe it as well is Munchausen syndrome by proxy.

> The only thing wrong with you is that you are easily convinced there is something wrong with you.
>
> RR

But let's not be so harsh. Let's assume there is something wrong with you and your child, and let's assume religion is the cure. How can you be sure your religion identifies the true dis-ease and hence offers the needed cure? No matter how ardently you chant the name of Lord Krishna, if the real dis-ease is sin and the real cure is Christ, you are doomed. And if you teach your children to worship Krishna rather than Christ, they too are doomed.

Before you make yourself and your family sick, question the entire dis-ease model of religion to see if there isn't a better way to live.

45
Doom of the Rock

Religion as Munchausen syndrome isn't only a private affair. Take, for example, the Temple Mount in Jerusalem.

This is the holiest place in Judaism and the third holiest in Islam. It is holy to Jews because this was where YHVH commanded the Jews to build their Second Temple. It is holy to Muslims because this was where the Prophet Muhammad (PBUH) rode his magical horse Buraq into the heavens to meet Allah and bring Islam to the world. The Muslim Dome of the Rock sits on the site of the long-demolished Second Temple.

Many Jews want to destroy the Dome of the Rock and rebuild the temple. Many more Muslims want to destroy the Jews if they try. Attempting either will trigger World War III.

Did YHVH really command the building of the temple in Jerusalem, or were the Jewish leaders of the southern kingdom of Judah seeking a monopoly on YHVH worship? Did Muhammad (PBUH) really ride a flying horse from Mecca to Jerusalem and from Jerusalem to heaven, or is this simply a story legitimizing Islamic practice?

If these are stories rather than histories, fighting over them is madness. And, in case you were wondering, they are stories.

> Tell people there's an invisible man in the sky who created the universe, and the vast majority will believe you. Tell them the paint is wet, and they have to touch it to be sure.
>
> often attributed to GEORGE CARLIN

46
What If Nothing's Wrong?

What if life is just the way it is because that is the only way it can be? What if, contrary to the narratives of brand-name religions, you are not subject to cosmic Ignorance, Exile, Original Sin, Endless Desire, or Pride? Not that you aren't sometimes ignorant, alienated, sinful, addicted, or proud, but that sometimes being ignorant, alienated, sinful, addicted, or proud has no cosmic significance and does not demand allegiance to any specific religion. If there's nothing wrong, religion as human meaning making won't disappear, but religion as Munchausen syndrome might.

We outgrow our Gods when we outgrow the dis-eases they promise to cure. If you want a better God, invent a better dis-ease.

RR

47
Here's What's Really Wrong with You

Here is what's really wrong with you: You imagine there
is something wrong with you. You imagine you should be
someone other than who you are. You imagine you should
live in the now when by the time you know it's now, that now
is already then. You imagine you can control your feelings
when you only know what you're feeling after you've already
felt it. You imagine you shouldn't have negative thoughts
when you only know what you're thinking after you've
thought it. You imagine you should not judge and then judge
yourself for judging.

What's wrong with you is that you are the result of 13.8
billion years of evolutionary trial and error and hence reflect
the inconsistencies and incongruities evolution contains. In
other words: what's wrong with you is that you are normal.

> Nobody wants to be normal. Everybody wants to be
> special. Since nobody's special, we imagine a God
> who says we're special: Chosen, Saved, True Believer,
> Enlightened, Awake, et cetera.   RR

48

Ordinary Holiness and Everyday Perfection

Jesus says, "Be perfect as your Father is perfect" (Matthew 5:48).

Jesus's God says, "I am the first and the last. Apart from me there is nothing else" (Isaiah 44:6) and "I am light and dark, prosperity and calamity. I, YHVH, am all of this" (Isaiah 45:7).

Being perfect as God is perfect doesn't mean being without flaw; it means being without lack. God is the entirety of reality—the negative along with the positive, evil along with good. Everything goes with its opposite, and God is all of it.

You are a manifesting of God. You too contain everything and its opposite. You too, as Walt Whitman sang, "contain multitudes."

To be perfect as God is perfect is to recognize your multitudes, to own your capacity for evil as well as your capacity for good, to realize that true perfection includes imperfection, to know that there is no way out of wholeness, and to rejoice in all humility that the Firesign Theatre prophets were right: "We're all bozos on this bus."

Nanakorobi yaoki: Fall down seven times. Get up eight. The only perfection you need.
RR

49
It Takes a Universe

Your very existence depends on your lungs and the oxygen they pump through your body. And while it is true that your body produces a variety of gases, oxygen isn't one of them. Plants and trees produce oxygen. If your existence depends on your lungs and your lungs depend on oxygen and oxygen depends on plants and trees, then plants and trees are you the same way your lungs are you. To produce oxygen, plants and trees need earth, water, and sunlight, so the earth, sky, and sun are also you. If plants and trees are to thrive, the sun and the earth need to maintain a certain distance from one another, and that requires the rest of the solar system to bend space just so. So the solar system too is your body.

As sparks arise from a blazing fire, so all beings arise from and return to the One.
Mundaka Upanishad 2.1.1

We could go on, and if we did, in time you would know that it takes a universe for you to be you.

50.
Why Are You Here?

You're here for the same reason everything else is here: you had no choice. You didn't choose to be here, because before you were here there was no you to do the choosing. You may imagine there was a you before you—a soul that existed before you and that will exist after you—but this is merely you fantasizing about always having been and always ever being you.

You are the result of 13.8 billion years of happenings over which you had no control. You are the latest blip in billions of other happenings over billions more years. But you are not irrelevant.

Your purpose is to understand the 13.8-billion-year process of which you are a part and to say, "WOW!" When you say, "WOW!" about the whole, you say, "WOW!" about each part, and when you say, "WOW!" about each part, you realize just how precious each part is. And when you realize just how precious each part is, you stop treating each part with anything but the deepest respect. And that is why you are here.

The seer cannot be seen,
the hearer cannot be heard,
the thinker cannot be thought,
the knower cannot be known.
This is your truest Self.
Brihadaranyaka Upanishad 3.4.2

51
Creative Bacteria

On the microscopic level, you are mostly bacteria. In fact, you comprise more bacterial cells than human ones. You might say you are the way bacteria write songs, marvel at sunsets, and invent stories for which you are willing to kill and die.

On the macroscopic level, you are more than 98 percent chimpanzee. That bit that isn't chimp allows you to climb out of the trees and walk on the moon, send probes up your butt and to the outer planets of our solar system, create reality television, and live in fantasy stories for which you are willing to kill and die.

On the cosmic level, you are the local expression of 13.8 billion years of evolutionary play, experimentation, accident, and surprise. Almost 14 billion years of play, and what do we have? Mostly rock. But look over here—chimps with nukes! How cool is that!

Yes, how cool is that?

52
Religion Noir

Individuals can be violent, but organized violence—war, genocide, apartheid, racism, et cetera—requires something special: a story.

Put toddlers in a playroom, and toddler A may bop toddler B on the head to take something that A wants and B has. But with enough time and indoctrination, teenager A will murder teenager B, not because of what B has, but because of who B is. A's understanding of who B is is a story.

Jerusalem matters to Jews, Christians, and Muslims, and they are willing to kill and die for her. But Hindus, Buddhists, Hopis, and secular atheists aren't. Why not? Jerusalem isn't part of their story.

"Humanity does not live on bread alone but on every word that comes from the mouth of YHVH" (Deuteronomy 8:3, Matthew 4:4). But every word that comes from the mouth of YHVH comes from the minds of those who write YHVH's story. We need bread. But we live and die on story.

> Very often when I talk to religious people and mention how important it is that compassion is the key, that it's the sine qua non of religion, people look kind of balked, and stubborn sometimes, as [if] to say, "What's the point of having religion if you can't disapprove of other people?"
>
> KAREN ARMSTRONG[9]

53
Dangerous Story

Religious stories can be catalogued in several binaries: those that bring us closer together and those that set us further apart; those that open our hearts and those that close them; those that broaden our circle of compassion and those that narrow it. Holy rascals challenge us to see which kinds of stories we are telling.

In *The King's Torah*, two Israeli rabbis, Yitzhak Shapira and Yosef Elitzur, argue that the commandment "Thou shalt not murder" (Exodus 20:13) applies only to Jews murdering Jews. Non-Jews, they write, are "uncompassionate by nature," and assaults on them "curb their evil inclination." They also argue that since the babies and children of Israel's enemies "will grow to harm us," they may be preemptively killed.[10] While Jews who did not share this story loudly opposed the book, *The King's Torah* was a best seller among those that did.

Holy rascals seek to subvert stories that trap us in fear, hate, ignorance, arrogance, and violence, and they try to help us tell new stories that lead to reconciliation, compassion, justice, and hospitality. Holy rascals undermine dangerous stories by revealing how the story serves the teller, often at the expense of the listener.

> With or without religion, you would have good people doing good things and evil people doing evil things.
> But for good people to do evil things, that takes religion.
>
> STEVEN WEINBERG[11]

54
Story Denial

The problem with religion isn't that it tells stories, but that it denies that the stories it tells are stories at all.

John Calvin (1509–64) told a story about a God who saves only a select few among us. This God—whom Calvin claimed was the only God—determined who would be saved and who would be damned prior to the creation of the world. Think about that for a moment. This means that God created most of humanity for the sole purpose of damning them to hell.

Who tells such a story? Calvinists tell this story because they believe being Calvinists proves they are among the saved.

Why believe in a God who creates most people for eternal damnation? Because doing so makes it all the more sweet to believe that you are not one of them.

Who can doubt that gunpowder against the infidel is incense for the Lord?
Gonzalo Fernández de Oviedo[12]

55
Drop the Story, Kill the God

Gods die when their stories stop masquerading as history. Gods die when people stop believing in the stories that support them. People stop believing in these stories when they no longer benefit from believing in them.

When Emperor Theodosius I made Christianity the official religion of the Roman Empire (380 CE), the old Gods found themselves out of a job. While some

Reclaiming metaphor and parable as metaphor and parable is an act of holy rascality. Insisting they are facts is an act of wholly insanity.

RR

pagans were forced to convert to Christianity, most did so as a matter of course. It simply made no sense to believe in stories and Gods who were no longer of benefit.

What happens to Gods when they die? Sometimes they are absorbed into another religion. Mars, for example, became Saint Martin of Mardi Gras, the Great Mars. Sometimes they return to what they originally were, the stuff of story, and the stories continue to be told, but no longer as history.

In our own time, dead Gods become psychological archetypes. Where the Goddesses and Gods once ruled over us, they now rule within us. Where once we told God's biography, we now use the Gods to tell our autobiography.

56
Reclaiming Metaphor and Parable

Holy rascals reinstate religion as a mechanism for making meaning by freeing parable from the prison of literalism. Doing so isn't easy: people are all too inclined toward the literal. Imagine what really happened when Jesus told the parable of the Good Samaritan (Luke 10: 25–37):

Jesus A man was going down from Jerusalem to Jericho when robbers attacked him.

Listener What was his name, Jesus? Why go from Jerusalem to Jericho? What the hell is there to do in Jericho?

J I don't know. Anyway, they took his clothes . . .

L What was he wearing? Was it nice stuff?

J . . . and they beat him senseless and left him for dead.

L Damn robbers! Where are those centurions when you need them?

J (*a bit exasperated*): Yeah, okay, I don't know. Anyway, a priest was going down the same road, and when he saw the man, he passed by on the other side.

Spectator 1: I think it was, "Blessed are the cheese makers."
Mrs. Gregory: Aha, what's so special about the cheese makers?
Gregory: Well, obviously it's not meant to be taken literally; it refers to any manufacturers of dairy products.

Monty Python's Life of Brian

L   *Bastard!* And what was he doing leaving Jerusalem? There's no temple in Jericho. Maybe he wasn't a priest at all. How do you know he was a priest, Jesus?

J   (*annoyed*): I don't know. It's a story. He was a priest. So then a Levite happened by and did the same thing.

L   What was his name? I'd like to report these guys.

J   I don't know their names; their names don't matter.

L   Why not? Are you saying all priests and Levites are heartless scoundrels? I'm down with that.

J   No, but a Samaritan—

L   A Samaritan! Those heretics! Why are you talking about them? Priests and Levites are bad enough!

J   Well, this Samaritan took pity on the man and bandaged his wounds, pouring on oil and wine.

L   Red wine or white wine? What wine goes with wounds? (*crowd laughs*)

J   (*angrily*): Don't be silly. He was trying to help the man.

L   By dousing him in alcohol? That's why I only go to Jewish doctors, even if a Samaritan is on my plan.

J   Then he put the man on his own donkey.

L   The man had a donkey? Why didn't the robbers take the donkey along with his clothes?

J   No, it was the Samaritan's donkey.

L   Oh. You have to be clear about these things.

J   Anyway, the Samaritan brought the man to an inn and took care of him.

> Anyone who thinks sitting in church can make you a Christian must also think that sitting in a garage can make you a car.
>
> commonly attributed to
> **Garrison Keillor**

L	What was the name of the inn?
J	I don't know.
L	I don't think there is an inn on the road to Jericho. Did someone build one recently? I haven't been to Jericho in ages. Not since my wife . . .
J	All right! Enough! Forget the story! Who's your neighbor? Your neighbor is someone who does nice things. OK? Get it?
L	The guy who lives next door to me is a schmuck. Does that mean he's not my neighbor?
J	Ahrrrrgh!

> [Jesus] speaks in parables, and though we have approached these parables reverentially all these many years and have heard them expounded as grave and reverent vehicles of holy truth, I suspect that many if not all of them were originally not grave at all but were antic, comic, often more than just a little shocking.
>
> FREDERICK BUECHNER, *Telling the Truth*

57
Parables, Not Proofs

When holy rascals talk about religion, we are talking about brand-name religions. While religion in and of itself is a way people make meaning out of the raw facts of our existence, one cannot point to "religion in and of itself," but only to specific religions, brand-name religions.

Each religion rests on a story, a narrative that "proves" the claims the religion makes about itself. If you accept the story as proof, you are a member of that religion. If you do not accept the story as proof, you are not a member, or at least not a member in good standing.

Holy rascals love the stories religions tell, but we read them as parables, not proofs. Parables are stories that impart wisdom regarding how things are and insight into how they might be. Proofs are stories that claim to be history and impart Truth. Holy rascals doubt the Truth claims of brand-name religions, but we are more than willing to mine their stories for wisdom.

The only true wisdom is knowing you know nothing.
Socrates

58
Mining a Parable

Jesus, a true holy rascal, said the kingdom of heaven is like a landowner who, having settled with workers on a day's wage, hired them early one morning to harvest his vineyard. He hired more workers midmorning, and did so again midafternoon, and again in the late afternoon. When the day's work was done, the landowner paid all his workers the full day's wage he had agreed upon with those he hired at dawn. Those who had labored for the entire day complained: Is it fair that those who worked only an hour or two be paid the same as those who worked a full day? The landlord explained that it was his money and he could do with it as he pleased.

Remember, the landlord represents the kingdom of heaven. If the parable ended here, Jesus's point would be that the kingdom is a socialist paradise where everyone receives the same pay no matter how much or how little work they do. Jesus doesn't end the parable here, however, but rather with the capping phrase "So the last will be first and the first will be last" (Matthew 20:16).

This sounds like a rebuke. In fact, it is the true revelation.

Parables speak on several levels at the same time.
For some, they are morality tales. For others, they
are extended metaphors or similes. For holy rascals
they are Molotov cocktails.　RR

59
No First, No Last

Everybody wants to be first; nobody wants to be last. But in Jesus's kingdom, the first will be last. But wait: the last will also be first, so the first will be first again as soon as they become last. But when they are once again first, they will immediately become last again, only to then become first again and then last again and first again and last again and first again until everybody is so dizzy that they drop the very notion of first and last. Which is the point.

> Religious people often prefer to be right rather than compassionate. . . . They don't want to give up their egotism, they want their religion to endorse their ego, their identity.
>
> KAREN ARMSTRONG[13]

60.
Belief versus Faith

Belief contains specific content: God is One, God is Three, God is Three Thousand; God cares about hats and whether or not women wear pants; God decides what you eat and whom you marry; God dictates books, chooses some people over others, and dabbles in real estate; God incarnates as a Hindu or a Jew; et cetera.

Faith has no content. Faith is an attitude: a willingness to see what is even as it changes into what is next. Faith is a practice: forever releasing what is in order to engage with what is next. Faith is the way of neti neti—"not this, not that"—which seeks to be true to Lao Tzu's idea that any God or religion that can be named, systematized, and peddled isn't the real thing.

If your faith leaves no room for doubt, you can be certain you are a prisoner of belief.
RR

Doubt and inquiry are the tools of faith. What we doubt is the content of belief. What we inquire into is the actual nature of reality.

While belief is essential to brand-name religion, you cannot make a brand out of faith.

61

Two Kinds of Doubt—Cheap and Costly

Cheap doubt says, "Since no belief can be proved, I choose to live without belief altogether."

Costly doubt says, "Because no belief can be proved and all beliefs are in service to some authority, I choose to live without authority altogether."

The holy rascal embodies costly doubt and chooses to live without taking refuge in this or that authority, tribe, -ism, or ideology. Going one step further than Immanuel Kant's *sapere aude*, "dare to know," the holy rascal dares to know that you cannot know and dares to live without knowing.

> I like the scientific spirit—the holding off, the being sure but not too sure, the willingness to surrender ideas when the evidence is against them: this is ultimately fine—it always keeps the way beyond open—always give life, thought, affection, the whole person, a chance to try over again after a mistake—after a wrong guess.
>
> WALT WHITMAN,
> *Walt Whitman's Camden Conversations*

62
Alright, Mr. DeMille,
I'm Ready for My Close-Up

The greatest authority is the God or Gods of brand-name religions. These Gods often speak to us through books interpreted by the lesser authorities empowered by the brand-name religions. Each brand has its own authority, and each authority takes refuge in the Great Authority it claims to represent. The holy rascal doubts the existence of the Great Authority of any brand-name religion and hence lives outside the authority of the lesser authorities upheld by each religion.

> The lifeblood of religiosity is questions. A religion with all the answers is dead and, worse, deadly.
>
> **RR**

Our outsider status gives us a unique position from which to question the claims of brand-name religions. Because we don't accept the premises of any religion, we can ask simple questions of those premises. For example, without denying the Christian notion that Christ died as ransom for our sins, the holy rascal might ask, "Why does God demand a ransom in the first place?" If God "so loved the world" (John 1:1), why not simply forgive everyone without going through the trouble of becoming human and dying on the cross on Calvary and then forgiving only those who believe the story and damning all those who don't?

Sometimes our questions upend a story. Take the story of the Ten Commandments, for example.

63
Climb Every Mountain

God commands the eighty-year-old Moses to make the hours-long climb to the summit of Mount Sinai. When Moses arrives, God tells him to go down and set boundaries around Mount Sinai to prevent the people from ascending or even touching its edge (Exodus 19:12). Moses does as commanded.

Three days later God again summons Moses to the mountaintop, and when he arrives, God again tells him to go back down and warn the people not to ascend the mountain (Exodus 19:20–21). Moses complains, reminding God that he had already issued this warning (Exodus 19:23). Realizing Moses has a point, God adds a new task: climb back down, tell the people what you already told them, and then climb back up, but this time bring your brother Aaron with you (Exodus 19:24).

Couldn't God have made this clear the first time? Of course he could have, and Moses knows it. Expecting the Israelites to question the sanity of their God and his fetish for mountain climbing, when Moses climbs down the mountain the second time, he preempts the questions by inventing ten commandments.

Wait! What?

64
Moses's Ten Suggestions

That can't be right. What about the forty days and forty nights on Mount Sinai? What about God writing the Ten Commandments on the tablets and Moses breaking them and then rewriting them? All of that happens in the Bible, but none of that happens here. Moses doesn't receive the Ten Commandments from God until Exodus 31, he doesn't shatter the tablets until Exodus 32, and he doesn't spend forty days and nights on Mount Sinai until Exodus 34. All that happens here is that Moses descends the mountain and says to the people, "God spoke all these words, saying . . ." (Exodus 19:25–20:1):

1 I am YHVH your God.

2 Have no other Gods besides Me, nor make graven images.

3 Do not take the name YHVH in vain.

4 Remember and observe the Sabbath.

5 Honor your father and mother.

6 Do not commit murder.

7 Do not commit adultery.

8 Do not steal.

9 Do not bear false witness.

10 Do not covet.

The problem isn't that these ten commandments are bad, but that God never commanded them. While Moses claims, "God spoke all these words," the Bible itself makes it clear that Moses is lying. While Moses makes this claim, God has said no such thing. All God said to Moses was that he should climb back down the mountain!

65

Take Two Tablets and Climb Back
Up to Me in a Few Chapters

Moses does get two tablets from God, but not for another
eleven chapters. "When YHVH finished speaking to Moses on
Mount Sinai, he gave him the two tablets, the covenant, two
tablets of stone inscribed by the finger of God" (Exodus 31:18).
Later, when Moses finds his people worshiping the golden
calf, he smashes the tablets (Exodus 32:19). God kills many
Israelites with a plague and then orders Moses to lead the
survivors to the Promised Land (Exodus 32:34–35). Days pass
before God tells Moses to "carve for yourself two stone tablets
like the first ones, and I shall inscribe on the tablets the words
that were on the first tablets, which you shattered" (Exodus
34:1). So Moses, carrying the two stone tablets, once more
treks up to the summit of Sinai, a journey that now includes
the distance the people have traveled since the plague. But at
last he is going to get the real Ten Commandments directly
from God, the very commandments that were inscribed on the
first set of tablets long after Moses's recitation of his own ten
commandments.

> Great spiritual books are filled with moments of cognitive
> dissonance: turning a conventional teaching on its head
> to get us to rethink its meaning. The problem is few of us
> read closely enough to get it.   RR

The Real Ten Commandments

1 Do not worship alien gods (Exodus 34:14).

2 Do not make molten gods for yourselves (Exodus 34:17).

3 Observe the Festival of Unleavened Bread (Exodus 34:18).

4 Dedicate the firstborn to God (Exodus 34:19).

5 Keep the Sabbath (Exodus 34:21).

6 Observe the festival of Shavuot/Pentecost (Exodus 34:22).

7 Observe Passover (Exodus 34:22).

8 Make three pilgrimages annually (Exodus 34:23).

9 Avoid eating leavened foods during Passover (Exodus 34:25).

10 Do not cook a calf in its mother's milk (Exodus 34:26).

These Ten Commandments listed in Exodus 34—and not those improvised by Moses in Exodus 19—are the true words of the covenant. How do we know? The Bible tells us so: "God then said to Moses, 'Write these words for yourself, for according to these words have I sealed a covenant with you and Israel.' Moses remained there with God for forty days and forty nights—he ate no bread and drank no water—and he wrote the words of the covenant, the Ten Commandments" (Exodus 34:27–28).

> If you think it would be impossible to improve upon the Ten Commandments . . . [read] Mahavira, the Jain patriarch: "Do not injure, abuse, oppress, enslave, insult, torment, torture, or kill any creature or living being."
>
> SAM HARRIS, *Letter to a Christian Nation*

66
The Two Most Dangerous Ideas

"God knows best" is the most dangerous idea we humans ever invented. "I know what God wants" is the second most dangerous.

The job of religious professionals is to extend the ramifications of their respective stories into the lives of their respective communities. It isn't enough to believe your story; you must live within the boundaries of the story as set by your religion's elite.

If you meet the Buddha on the road, kill him.
Linji Yixuan, Tang Dynasty Ch'an Master

The reason Jews are forbidden to eat pork has nothing to do with lack of refrigeration and the danger of trichinosis in Moses's time. The reason Jews are forbidden to eat pork is because their story—and their God—says so. While many Jews substitute trichinosis for Torah in order to justify eating pork by pointing out that Jews today have refrigerators, the fact is their love of pork is stronger than their loyalty to Torah. Trichinosis is just an excuse for eating a BLT with extra mayo and no guilt.

If you meet the Buddha on the road, warn him about Linji Yixuan.
RR

67
The Work of the Holy Rascal

The God of the holy rascal is the God beyond brands. To paraphrase Lao Tzu: the God that can be branded is not the true God. The religion of the holy rascal is the religion beyond brands, religion as art in service to meaning making.

The holy rascal doesn't want to erase brand-name Gods and religions, only to make it clear how they operate. Our job isn't to dethrone the emperor, only to point out that the emperor has no clothes. Our task isn't to banish the Great and Terrible Wizard, only to reveal that the Land of Oz is run by a small man with a large megaphone. Our work isn't to demolish the stories people tell, but to show them to be parables rather than histories and in this way free those who love them from being exploited by them.

The God of your understanding is just that: the God of your understanding. What you need is the God just beyond your understanding.

RR

68
Free Prize Inside

One way our religious professionals keep us attached to their story is to promise a prize to those who stay.

Christianity's promise is "Be faithful unto death, and I will give you a crown of life" (Revelation 2:10).

Islam promises that in heaven male believers get the companionship of full-breasted women of their own age (Qur'an 78:33). Women, on the other hand, only get one man with whom they will be satisfied.

My aim is to find myself in Dante's first circle of hell. That's where all the cool people are.

RR

Unlike Christianity and Islam, Judaism's prize was originally this-worldly: seasonal rains, abundant harvests, and fat cows (Deuteronomy 11:13–15). Jewish religious leaders shifted to a prize offered in the afterlife when the people noticed that the weather wasn't cooperating.

As it turns out, the best prize is one you collect after you die. That way, if it turns out there is no prize and your history was, in fact, just a story, you can't complain to the elite or warn the masses. You're dead.

69
FTTT

The operating system of most religions is called FTTT, or FT3: "First This, Then That." Here is a classic example from the Hebrew Bible:

> If you scrupulously observe the commands I am giving you—love God and serve God with all your heart and soul—then I will grant you rains in their proper seasons, and bountiful harvests, and abundant grasses for your cattle, and you will eat and be satisfied (Deuteronomy 11:13–15).

In order to reap the reward God promises, you must do what God commands: First This, Then That. Of course, to help encourage you to pursue the carrot, FT3 also comes with an equally powerful stick:

> But beware! If you allow yourselves to be seduced by other Gods, to worship them and bow down to them, God's wrath will turn against you: the sky will not yield its rain, the earth will fall lifeless, and you will swiftly die even on this good land God has given you (Deuteronomy 11:16–17).

 Defending himself in court, the accused writes a note and hands it to the judge, saying, "This proves my innocence." The note reads, "I am innocent." The accused is a theologian.   RR

70.

Pascal's Wager

The French philosopher Blaise Pascal (1623–62) argued that to believe in God and follow God's dictates is rational because not doing so could be hazardous to your eternal soul.

Let's say there is no God, and yet you choose to believe otherwise. When you die, what will you lose? True, you will gain no reward, and in life you did give up whatever pleasures your God said were forbidden. But these are mere trifles compared to what you will lose if there is a God and you choose not to believe and therefore suffer eternal damnation after you die. Since you cannot know if God exists or not, it is only reasonable to hedge your bets and believe.

Every religion is true . . . when understood metaphorically. But when it gets stuck in its own metaphors, interpreting them as facts, then you are in trouble.
Joseph Campbell, *The Power of Myth*

The problem with Pascal's wager is that he assumes there is only one God (the Holy Trinity) and only one religion (the Catholic Church). But in a world where there are multiple Gods and thousands of religions, even if you stipulate that it is more rational to believe than not to believe, you still have no idea in what or in whom to believe. There are too many Gods, too many religions, and no way to know which, if any, is the true God and religion. Thus the rational person is frozen into inaction and nonbelief.

71
What Happens to You When You Die?

What happens to you when you die? Nothing. You're dead. You are a temporary manifesting of a singular reality: God, Brahman, Nature, the Universe, Mother, the Happening happening as all happening. When you die, the unique manifesting that is you ceases to be, but manifesting continues—just not as you.

Our obsession with the afterlife reflects our addiction to this life, to this particular manifesting we identify as "me." But if we identify with the whole rather than the part, the need for an afterlife is moot.

We cling to notions of an afterlife for the same reason we cling to notions of this life: we simply can't accept the fact that in the eyes of the universe we are no more special than a slug.

RR

72

Is There Life after Beach?

Imagine you're standing on the seashore listening to the waves as they become aware of the approaching rocky shoreline. Their talk is about one thing and one thing only: *Is there life after beach?* Some say no, others say yes, but you know what the waves do not: they are the ocean, and the ocean keeps on waving.

You are a temporary manifesting of Reality the way a wave is a temporary manifesting of the ocean. Not knowing this is a form of seasickness.

RR

What is true of waves is true of you. You are a unique, precious, temporary, and never-to-be-repeated manifesting of the universe (or God, if you like). And when you die, your particular manifesting ends, but the greater manifesting of which you are a part goes on.

73
To Be or Knot to Be

Imagine you're holding a foot-long piece of cotton rope. Tie a knot in the rope. Is the knot different from or other than the rope? No. The knot is simply a configuration of the rope.

Tie a second knot in the rope. Does this second knot differ from the first? Yes. It is in a different location, and it may be tighter or looser or larger or smaller than the first. Is the second knot different from or other than the rope? No. Both knots are the same rope.

The Dalai Lama has fourteen lives. Cats have nine. Mrs. Katz has only one. Is she the poorer for it?

RR

Now imagine the first knot is you and the second, a loved one. Untie the second knot. Where did it go? Nowhere. And yet it is gone. And to the extent you loved that knot—its unique shape and texture and "personality"—you will grieve over its loss. But, again, where did it go? Where could it go? The beloved knot is the rope, and the rope is still there.

While it is common and right to grieve over a beloved knot that is no longer, to imagine it somehow exists separate from the rope is to misunderstand the very nature of knots in the first place.

74
Enjoy the Strawberries

To rid themselves of a troublesome lion who'd gotten a taste for human flesh, a team of villagers dig a pit, fit the bottom with razor-sharp bamboo spikes, and cover the top with thatch. When the lion walks over the thatch, he will fall to his death, skewered on the spikes. Unexpectedly, however, a man from a neighboring village falls into the pit instead. To save himself from the spikes, he grabs hold of a vine, planning to pull himself up and climb out. Just then, the lion appears. Frozen in fear, the man clings to the vine. At that moment, a mole pops out and begins gnawing at the vine beyond the man's reach. His fate sealed, the man notices a strawberry growing on the vine. He plucks the fruit and eats it, saying, "This is the finest strawberry I have ever tasted!"

You are this villager. There is no escape from the pit. The only thing that matters is this: *Can you enjoy the strawberry?* Most of us can't. Most of us call for help, curse the vine, curse the mole, curse the Gods or fate or our parents, spouse, boss, or friends. Most of us never notice the strawberry, let alone taste it.

The power of a parable is its ability to reveal the truth before you have time to think about it.
RR

Holy rascals want to change that.

75
Being Zusha

Religion and death go together. In fact, if it were not for death, people might not have invented religion. That's because religion is a way we humans make meaning out of the raw facts of our existence, and death is the rawest fact of all.

Lying on his deathbed, Rabbi Zusha of Hanipol reportedly said, "Our sages command us to be as great as Moses, yet Torah tells us no one can be as great as Moses [Deuteronomy 34:10]. If, when I die, God asks me, 'Why were you not like Moses?' I know what to say. But this is not God's question. God's question is 'Why were you not yourself?' And to this I will have nothing to say."

Being yourself means being the unique manifesting of Reality you already are instead of conforming to the ideal set for you by someone else.

Of course, this does allow for sociopaths and psychopaths, and that is the challenging part of Reality: it makes room for everything. Jeffrey Dahmer is no less God than Mother Teresa. It's just that when he says he'd like to have you over for dinner, you should decline the offer.

If, when I die, I have the opportunity to choose my fate, I would choose this: not to be dead.

RR

76
After Me

Some people imagine that you are not a self but a soul and that it is the soul and not the self that reincarnates on earth or rejoices in heaven or suffers in hell. This is a distinction without a difference. Almost everyone who imagines going to heaven thinks that the person going there is the person they take themselves to be here on earth. If it isn't me that goes to heaven but, rather, some other being about whom I know nothing and yet who is supposed to be the real me, where is the reward?

When we imagine reuniting with loved ones in heaven, we imagine them as we remember them, and not as some nondescript soul that doesn't look, smell, feel, sound, or act like them. The same is true with hell. When we fantasize about this or that person burning forever in hell, we want the person suffering to be the person we know, and not some soul stand-in.

So even when we say our true self isn't the self we see in the mirror, we don't really believe it.

> In order that the happiness of the saints may be more delightful to them and that they may render more copious thanks to God for it, they are allowed to see perfectly the sufferings of the damned. . . . So that they may be urged the more to praise God . . . the saints in heaven know distinctly all that happens . . . to the damned.
>
> SAINT THOMAS AQUINAS, *Summa Theologica*

77
I'll Be Back

The same is true regarding reincarnation. If the soul, or atman, that migrates from life to life isn't me, then what's the point? If my soul has to suffer a horrible incarnation in the next life to atone for some terrible crime I committed in this life and that soul isn't me, then the entire system is unjust. If I look at a destitute person living on the sidewalk and say that this is his just reward for some past-life transgression, the long-dead transgressor and the currently living homeless person must be one and the same, or the system is capricious and evil.

Holy rascals don't have any more insight into what happens when we die than anyone else. What makes you a holy rascal isn't that you know something others don't, but that you ask questions others won't.

Chuang Tzu asked: "Am I a man dreaming I'm a butterfly, or am I a butterfly dreaming I'm a man?"

Actually it was a hookah-smoking caterpillar dreaming them both.　RR

78
Enlightenment

Imagine finding yourself in a pitch-black room filled with dangerous obstacles, pitfalls, and traps. You literally cannot see your hand in front of your face, and yet you have no choice but to move through the room searching for an exit that may or may not exist. This is the unenlightened state.

Now imagine yourself in the same room with the same dangers and the same need to find an exit that may or may not exist, except this time you have a penlight with you. This is the enlightened state.

The room is your life. The darkness arises from your sense of being apart from, rather than a part of, Reality, God, Tao, Nature, et cetera. The obstacles are what the Buddha called the suffering of birth, sickness, old age, and death. The enlightened and unenlightened face the same existential reality. The only difference is the quality of their navigation.

It isn't by getting out of the world that we become enlightened, but by getting into the world . . .
by getting so tuned in that we can ride the waves of our existence and never get tossed because we become the waves.

KEN KESEY, *Kesey's Garage Sale*

79

Enlightenment Is in the I of the Beholder

The difference between being enlightened and being unenlightened isn't the presence or absence of ego, but the place the ego occupies in your life. After all, if you lacked all sense of self, who would wipe your butt and keep you from wiping someone else's?

The ego, the self that imagines itself apart from rather than a part of the Happening that is happening as all happening, is a tool for navigating the world as it appears to us in our normal waking state. The goal isn't to kill the self but to be freed from the self and to place the self in service to the Self.

The true value of human beings can be found in the degree to which they have attained liberation from the self.
Albert Einstein, *Ideas and Opinions*

If we exaggerate this self, we catastrophize its experience and seek to escape from it through the pursuit of enlightenment, heaven, or a superior rebirth. But if we allow the ego to do what it does best, and not get trapped in its hyperbolic notions of itself, we are never apart from and always a part of Reality. We recognize the uniqueness and preciousness of every I without imagining that they are other than the singular I'*ing* that is all. And when we do this, we treat all beings justly and compassionately, and we become a blessing to all the families of the earth (Genesis 12:3). That's enlightenment.

Or if it's not, enlightenment is irrelevant.

80.
Zeno's Enlightenment

Zeno of Elea (490–430 BCE) was a pre-Socratic Greek philosopher famous for Zeno's paradox: in seeking to move from point A to point B, you must first reach point ½ B, and to do that you must first reach ½ ½ B, and to do that you must first reach ½ ½ ½ B, and so on, proving that you can never actually reach point B. Rumor has it that Zeno articulated this paradox in response to his wife's query, "Zeno, did you take out the garbage yet?" He hadn't and tried to explain why.

Zeno's paradox speaks to those of us searching for enlightenment. Many of us look to a method for awakening, a practice that will bring us to enlightenment. As long as we devote ourselves to a practice that will bring us to enlightenment in the future, we will never be enlightened in the present.

Practice distracts us from awakening now by promising us awakening later. This is not an argument against practice, only an argument against practicing for some goal. Sit, chant, and pray because you love to sit, chant, and pray. Enlightenment will take care of itself.

> Let me tell you how
> to become enlightened.
> No!
> Wait!
> First let me tell you . . .
> No!
> Wait! . . .   RR

81
Life One, Phase One

The Hebrew Bible tells us that the matriarch Sarah "lived one hundred years, and twenty years, and seven years; these are the years of Sarah's life" (Genesis 23:1). The ancient rabbis taught that "these are the years of Sarah's life" can also be read as "these are the two lives of Sarah." Sarah represents each of us. We each live two lives. Life One consists of two phases: one long and one short. Life Two is shorter still.

Life One, Phase One is a life of material consumption. This is similar to the Hindu life stages *brahmacharya* (student) and *grihastha* (householder). Our goal is to master the knowledge and skills we need in order to accumulate the stuff we desire: job, spouse, children, houses, cars, clothes, and the latest iPhone. Eventually we achieve our goals, and yet we find ourselves dissatisfied. The question "Is this all there is?" haunts us. Some of us respond to this question by accumulating more stuff. But many of us realize that no car is going to bring us deep satisfaction (well, no car we can afford anyway), and so we move on to Life One, Phase Two.

> It's not that God doesn't want to give you things, it's that the things God wants to give you you can't use, like grass for your cattle (Deuteronomy 11:15) when your dwelling isn't zoned for cows.   RR

82
Life One, Phase Two

Life One, Phase Two is similar to the third of Hinduism's
four life stages, *vanaprastha* (forest dweller), when we devote
ourselves to spiritual matters. Similar, but not identical. Where
the Hindu leaves accumulation behind, devotees of Life
One, Phase Two simply transfer their accumulating from the
secular to the spiritual. We pursue the spiritual with the same
mindset with which we pursued the material. We collect gurus,
initiations, spiritual books, icons, music, and films; buy the
very best yoga mats, meditation cushions, yoga clothes, malas,
and prayer shawls; and attend as many meditation retreats and
visit as many holy sites as our schedules and budgets permit.
And in the end, when we are stuffed with stuff of the spirit, the
question returns, "Is this all there is?"

> I traveled to India to study with the forest dwellers. I
> packed the finest lululemon yoga clothes and carried the
> best Manduka yoga mat. The yogis I met were naked,
> with stones tied to their balls with string. I asked them
> where to buy the finest stones and the best string.   RR

83
It's All about Me

Both phases of Life One are all about "me," the self you take yourself to be when you're trapped in the illusion of being apart from the Happening that is happening as all happening rather than realizing that you're a happening of the Happening happening.

This illusion can be very subtle, and lots of us enamored with Life One, Phase Two are convinced that we are beyond the self, that we have dropped the "me" and now rest in the infinite I'*ing* of God.

Chances are anyone who confesses to being enlightened is lying—to you, to themselves, and most likely both.

What makes enlightened people seem special is that they are so very ordinary, while all the rest of us are desperately trying to be anything but.

RR

84

LIFE ONE, PHASE TWO   Confession

Taking a walk during a silent meditation retreat, I stood
on a bridge and observed the river flowing beneath me.
Something was wrong. It seemed to me that the river's rocks
and logs were not in proper
aesthetic alignment to one
another. I climbed down the
embankment, waded into
the water, and began to
rearrange them.

*Last night, deep in meditation,
I lost the world and gained
the universe. But still I lost
the world and had to replace
it in the morning. It cost me
an arm and a leg.*

RR

I'd shift a few rocks and
logs, then climb up to the
bridge to judge the result.
Not satisfied, I'd climb
back into the river to try
again. I did this for a very long time.

Drenched and tired, I eventually took a break on the
riverbank. And then it hit me: everything is as it should be,
and meddling is a reflection of ego. And then I laughed. I
laughed at myself, of course, but mostly I laughed at my fellow
seekers who thought they could get enlightened sitting on
a cushion when in fact you had to rearrange the river. Then
I stopped laughing and began working on how to market
Rearranging the River™ spiritual retreats.

85

LIFE TWO   Reality and All That Jazz

Having accumulated as much as we could both materially and spiritually, we are exhausted. And still the question haunts us: Is this all there is? The answer is still no, but we just can't muster the energy to buy one more book, attend one more retreat, check out one more guru, or make one more pilgrimage. With a great sigh, we resign ourselves to never waking up, never achieving enlightenment. We lived Life One with the motto "Get it!" We end Life One with the motto "F#ck it!" And when we do, the "it" falls away, and we enter Life Two.

Life Two may be compared to Hinduism's fourth stage, *sannyasa*, the stage of renunciation. In Life Two we switch on the penlight and see what is with a new clarity. In Life Two the obstacles are no less, but we can navigate them so much more effectively. We are no longer in opposition to anything but are, rather, in harmony with everything.

It isn't that we no longer have desires; it's that we are no longer driven by them, especially the desire to have no more desires. It isn't that reality suddenly makes sense to us; it's that making sense no longer makes sense to us.

> Life One, Phase One is like Charlie Brown aiming for the football Lucy is holding: you kick and fall and kick and fall, hoping next time she won't pull the ball away. In Life One, Phase Two, you kick and fall and kick and fall, believing she is teaching you something important by pulling the ball away. In Life Two, you kick and fall and kick and fall for the joy of kicking and falling.   RR

86
All Is One and One Is All

The world is wild, chaotic, free, whole, broken, awesome, awful, wonderful, and ultimately nondual—a huge canvas on which we are both painting and being painted. This is what the Buddhists call *pratītyasamutpāda*, "dependent origination": everything is dependent upon and interconnected with everything else. This is what M. C. Escher illustrates in his 1948 lithograph *Drawing Hands*, in which each hand holds a pen and is drawing the other. This is the *taijitu*, or yin-yang symbol, of the Taoists showing the complementarity and interconnection of seeming opposites. This is Jesus's teaching that to enter the Kingdom of Heaven one must "make the two one, and the inner like the outer and the outer like the inner, and the upper like the lower, and male and female into a single one" (Gospel of Thomas logion 22).

 There is no rhyme or reason, only a continuous and continuously repeating chord progression— Pranava, the hum of reality—played by the rhythm section of the universe and over which you improvise your own fresh melodies.   RR

87
Möbius World

The world is a Möbius strip where the appearance of in and out, this and that, one thing and another yields the simple truth of Only This. You can see this for yourself:

1   Take a sheet of printer paper and cut a two-inch-wide strip off the long side. Lay the strip out horizontally and label the corners: upper left is 1, upper right is 2, lower left is 3, and lower right is 4.

2   Pick up the strip and put a half twist in it so that the numbers 1 and 3 face you while the numbers 2 and 4 face away from you.

3   Bring the ends of the strip together so corner 1 sits on corner 4 and corner 2 sits on corner 3. Tape or staple the ends together and you have a Möbius strip.

At any given point on the Möbius strip, the strip appears to be two-sided, but this is an illusion. Take a marker and draw a horizontal line on the strip without lifting the marker from the paper. In a moment you will cover the entire strip and end up where you started, thus proving that the Möbius strip is in fact one-sided.

The same is true of the universe: while it appears to be a collection of opposites, in fact there is only the One.

Before enlightenment: chop wood, carry water.
After enlightenment: chop wood, carry water.
Skip enlightenment: invest in a gas stove and
indoor plumbing.   RR

88
Acceptance

Accept whatever comes your way. Don't resist, don't avoid, don't ignore—just accept what is and move on to what is next.

Don't buy into the notion that you can or should control your own reality. Given the interdependence of all events, for you to control your reality, you must also control everyone else's reality, and if you even entertain such an idea, you are trapped in the hyperinflation of self, a narcissistic world view that leaves you feeling victimized by reality even as you imagine yourself in charge of reality.

You can't change what is, since it already is what is. But you can impact what is next by what you do with what is.

> While some people like to say, "I create my own reality," what they're really saying is, "I can't stand reality, so I'll take refuge in my own fantasy." This is good news for those selling books, CDs, and workshops on how to create your own reality, but bad news for those who are spending serious money buying them.   RR

89
Einstein Is Wrong

Albert Einstein said God doesn't play dice with the universe. Either Einstein was wrong, or I don't understand what he was saying. I assume Einstein was wrong.

The law of probability governs every throw of the dice: sevens and elevens come up far more often than twos and twelves. If the universe were random, this would not be the case. But it isn't random. It is governed by probabilities, and the probability of throwing a seven is always greater than the probability of throwing a two. Respecting the fact that this moment is not an accident but, rather, the result of conditions playing out both in and as this moment frees you from imagining that you are in control of any of it.

There is little over which you have control. But one thing over which you do have control is the notion that you have control. You don't. So take control and stop saying you are in control.   RR

90.
Don't Detach—Engage

Enlightened people are not detached from life; they are detached from the illusion they are in control of life.

While many spiritual people speak of being detached as a sign of their spiritual maturity or (God forbid) enlightenment, what they are really saying is that life sucks so badly they don't want anything to do with it. While it may make sense to step back and not be controlled by your desires, feelings, thoughts, and Twitter trolls, it makes no sense to detach from life itself.

As Lao Tzu would have tweeted, "Do your work, then step back. The only way to tranquility" (*Tao Te Ching* 9).

And as would-be bodhisattvas chant, *Shu jo mu hen sei gan do*: "Though sentient beings are innumerable, I vow to save them all."

And as the first-century sage Rabbi Tarfon taught, "It's not your responsibility to complete the work [of perfecting the world], but neither are you free to abstain from it" (*Pirkei Avot* 2:21).

Living an enlightened life means respectfully engaging with what is and then doing your best to make what is next a bit more loving, kind, peaceful, and just.

The only difference between ordinary living and enlightened living is the notion there is a difference between ordinary living and enlightened living.

RR

91
Don't Ask

There is one question holy rascals never ask: How can you be so stupid as to believe this nonsense?

Everyone is trapped in one story or another, even if that story is the story that you are not trapped in one story or another. To imagine that your story is true and the other's false, or to imagine you are free while the other is trapped, simply perpetuates the problem and does nothing to solve it.

The difference between belief and faith is simple: belief is something you hold onto; faith is what remains when you have nothing left to hold.
RR

The problem is belief itself: accepting some -ism or ideology as true without requiring a shred of evidence proving it is true. The alternative to belief is faith: a radical openness to what is without knowing in advance what is.

Belief keeps us from faith by distracting us from reality. The more we insist reality is what we say it is, the less we can engage with reality as it really is.

92
Do Ask

There is one question holy rascals always ask, though we rarely ask it abstractly: Can you laugh at what you believe?

Our goal isn't to make fun of what others believe or to mock those who believe it, but to skillfully pull back the curtain that masks the absurdities of belief systems and that protects those who benefit from them. If people can laugh at their beliefs, they have taken a huge step toward freeing themselves from them. As Alan Watts once said, "Real religion is the transformation of anxiety into laughter."[14]

> Perhaps the mission of those who love mankind is to make people laugh at the truth, *to make the truth laugh*, because the only truth lies in learning to free ourselves from insane passion for the truth.
>
> UMBERTO ECO, *The Name of the Rose*

93
Relativism

Relativism is the notion that all beliefs are culturally biased constructs rather than independent and absolute truths. In the minds of many, however, *relativism* has come to mean that all beliefs are equal and that none is better or more true than any other.

We use *relativism* in its original meaning: while it is true that all beliefs are culturally conditioned, it is not true that all beliefs are equally valid, viable, or worth believing. Beliefs that close minds, harden hearts, and tighten fists are to be challenged and rejected. Those that open minds, soften hearts, and unclench fists are worthy of celebration.

[Humans] are the only animal that has the True Religion—several of them.
Mark Twain, *The Wit and Wisdom of Mark Twain*

94
Play

Holy rascals are playful and lighthearted. While our task is serious—the liberation of humanity from the madness of unhealthy and harmful religions and religious beliefs—our attitude is not.

Partly this is strategic: nobody wants to listen to a pompous blowhard wailing against religion, especially if the religion being attacked is your own. And partly this is intrinsic to the work: we are humorists, clowns, fools, and incapable of taking ourselves too seriously.

If you find yourself taking all of this too seriously, give yourself a break. Visit a cathedral and marvel at the architecture. Go to church, temple, mosque, or synagogue and get carried away by the music and theater. Remind yourself that you are not the scourge of religion, but a lover of religion who just wants to free it and the religious from the rust that accrues on it. You are to religion what cleaner fish are to the fish they clean: one that removes what is dead and deadly so the living fish can thrive.

The fact that play and culture are actually interwoven with one another was neither observed nor expressed, whereas for us the whole point is to show that genuine, pure play is one of the main bases of civilization.

JOHAN HUIZINGA,
Homo Ludens: A Study of the Play-Element in Culture

95
Not-Knowing

Holy rascals need to keep an open mind without falling into the trap of being empty-headed. While we are curious about what people believe, we are not looking to add to our own beliefs. On the contrary, we are interested in cultivating faith in the contentless engagement with what is, and not in accumulating beliefs that distract us from what is by focusing our attention on what someone insists must be.

Not-knowing is not the same as ignorance. Ignorance is the absence of knowledge when knowledge can be known. Not-knowing is an abundance of knowing that the knowledge we seek cannot be known. Brand-name religions are selling you the known; holy rascals give away not-knowing for free.

Religion in so far as it is a source of consolation is a hindrance to true faith: in this sense atheism is a purification.
Simone Weil, Gravity and Grace

Hacking the
HOLY

Theology should be like poetry, which takes us
to the end of what words and thoughts can do.
Karen Armstrong[15]

96
Spiritual Culture Jamming

Spiritual culture jamming is an act of subvertising.
Subvertising in a religious context appropriates the imagery
and language of brand-name religion to undercut its claims to
truth. That is to say, we don't simply deny the truth claims of
any given religion: we play with them, we hack them, we push
them to their absurdist conclusions in order to free people
from taking them literally.

> Reckless and incompetent expounders of Holy Scripture
> bring untold trouble and sorrow on their wiser brethren
> when they are caught in one of their mischievous false
> opinions and are taken to task by those not bound by the
> authority of our sacred books. For then to defend their
> utterly foolish and obviously untrue statements they will
> try to call upon Holy Scripture for proof and even recite
> from memory many passages which they think support their
> position although they understand neither what they say nor
> the things about which they make assertion (1 Timothy 1:7).
>
> SAINT AUGUSTINE, *The Literal Meaning of Genesis*

97
Mockery versus Satire

Religulous is Bill Maher's 2008 documentary on the absurdity of religion. *Life of Brian* is Monty Python's 1979 take on religion and the life of Jesus in particular. While both movies have fun at religion's expense, only *Life of Brian* is an act of holy rascality.

Religulous mocks believers; *Life of Brian* challenges the nature of belief. *Religulous* equates religion with literalism; *Life of Brian* takes aim at literalism and says that this is what religion can, but should not, become. *Religulous* scoffs at religion and the religious; *Life of Brian* satirizes religion and the religious.

Spiritual culture jamming aims for the satire of *Life of Brian* and seeks to avoid the mockery of *Religulous*.

Bill Maher   You are one of the very few people who are actually running this country. It worries me that people are running my country who believe in a talking snake.

Senator Mark Pryor   You don't have to pass an IQ test to be in the Senate, though. (*chuckles*) (from *Religulous*)

And there shall in that time be rumours of things going astray, and there will be a great confusion as to where things really are, and nobody will really know where lieth those little things with the sort of raffia work base, that has an attachment. . . . At this time, a friend shall lose his friend's hammer and the young shall not know where lieth the things possessed by their fathers that their fathers put there only just the night before around eight o'clock . . .

BORING PROPHET, *Monty Python's Life of Brian*

98
Memes to an End

Religious memes are images, ideas, and texts carried by story, theology, ritual, symbol, and music that shape our thinking about God, self, other, morality, ethics, life, and the afterlife. Holy rascals subvert religious memes to disrupt unthinking acquiescence to whatever it is a religion posits as true. Our goal isn't to dismiss the memes of religion but to encourage people to think about them critically by looking at them humorously.

Potent memes can change minds, alter behavior . . . and transform cultures. . . . Whoever has the memes has the power.

Kalle Lasn, *Culture Jam*

99
The Good, the Bad, and the Ugly

Religion is never impartial. It either liberates or it enslaves; it either empowers or it disempowers. A good religion liberates, empowers, and points beyond itself toward the greater Reality no religion can own. A bad religion enslaves, disempowers, and points only to itself, becoming, not a means to an end, but an end unto itself. An ugly religion enslaves, disempowers, points only to itself, and breaks the fingers of those who point anywhere else.

Spiritually culture jamming bad religion reveals the meme behind the elites who use religious memes to control others and empower themselves. Spiritually culture jamming ugly religion shatters the veil of goodness that masks the evil done in the name of God.

> When a population becomes distracted by trivia, when cultural life is redefined as a perpetual round of entertainments, when serious public conversation becomes a form of baby-talk, when, in short, a people become an audience and their public business a vaudeville act, then a nation finds itself at risk; culture-death is a clear possibility.
>
> NEIL POSTMAN, *Amusing Ourselves to Death*

100.
The Religion That Cannot Be Branded

Spiritual culture jammers aren't religious reformers seeking
to adapt ancient mores to contemporary sense and sensibility.
Nor are we religious revolutionaries seeking to overthrow
conventional religion and replace it with a brand of our own.
We are religious anarchists and spiritual subversives whose
goal is to free religion from branding altogether and, in this
way, to set meaning making free so humans can imagine
new ways of being holy that do not fall into the clutches of
tribalism and its passion for demonizing the other.

In a small room where people unanimously
maintain a conspiracy of silence,
one word of truth sounds like a pistol shot.
Czeslaw Milosz[16]

101
The Art of the Aphorism

We live in the Twitterverse: a world saturated with information—some accurate, some inaccurate; some of it deep and compelling, much of it shallow and mind-numbing. We live in a world where critical thinking is discouraged, leading some of us to cling to ideologies without reflection or to reject all thought as mere ideology. We live in a world where propaganda passes for truth and cleverness is mistaken for wisdom.

This isn't going to change any time soon.

If holy rascals are to pierce the fog of information and reach people with our ideas, we must be brief, clear, and compelling in our presentation. In short (pun intended), we must master the art of the aphorism: writing short "to hold the swift insights and fresh observations that are the raw data of the wisdom of the ages".[17]

Aphorisms are literature's hand luggage. Light and compact, they fit easily into the overhead compartment of your brain and contain everything you need to get through a rough day at the office or a dark night of the soul.
James Geary, *The World in a Phrase*

102
Five Laws of a Successful Aphorism

In his magnificent study of all things aphorismic, *The World in a Phrase*, James Geary offers us the five laws of writing powerful aphorisms:

1 Aphorisms must be brief.

2 Aphorisms must be definitive.

3 Aphorisms must be personal.

4 Aphorisms must have a twist.

5 Aphorisms must be philosophical.

> Friedrich Nietzsche's ambition was "to say in ten sentences what everyone else says in a book—what everyone else *does not* say in a book." Our ambition is to be briefer still.   RR

1. Aphorisms Must Be Brief
Forget the thirty-second elevator speech: you've got *five seconds* to make your point. Take a moment and count them off: one Mississippi, two Mississippi, three Mississippi, four Mississippi, five Mississippi—buzzer sounds! Time's up! Put your pencil down. That's it.

Aphorisms must work quickly because they are meant for times of emergencies.
James Geary, *The World in a Phrase*

But wait! I have so much more to say!

Maybe so, but people don't have the time to listen to you say it.

"Aphorisms are like particle accelerators for the mind," explains Geary. "When high-energy particles like electrons and positrons collide inside an accelerator, new particles are created as the energy of the crash is converted into matter. . . . Inside an aphorism, it is minds that collide, and the new matter that spins out at the speed of thought is that elusive thing we call wisdom."[18]

What's the emergency? People are drowning in a sea of nonsense and need a life raft now!
RR

2. Aphorisms Must Be Definitive

Aphorisms assert a truth rather than argue a position. When writing an aphorism, don't bother to persuade; simply state the matter as you see it. Dare to be wrong. And don't be afraid to be right. Don't second-guess yourself. Don't hedge, hem, or haw.

Of course there is more to say on the matter than what you can say in five seconds. This isn't a doctoral dissertation; it's a new meme intended to subvert the dominant meme by offering something no less assertive and compelling in its place. Your goal isn't to get people to agree with you, but to invite them to think with you and for themselves.

For example, take the road sign "Jesus is the answer." In just four words the aphorism affirms a simple belief without bogging you down in centuries of theological argument. Now hack the sign: "Jesus is the answer. But are you asking the right question?" With this slight twist (see law number 4) you invite people to think, to put their beliefs under the microscope of reflection. And this is what spiritual culture jamming is all about.

> Aphorisms are not bits of uplifting text meant for passive consumption. They are challenging statements that demand a response: either the recognition of a shared insight . . . or a rejection and retort.
>
> JAMES GEARY, *The World in a Phrase*

3. Aphorisms Must Be Personal

Your aphorisms articulate your wisdom. Write only what you hold to be true, not simply what you think is clever.

When someone asks, "Do you really mean this?" regarding an aphorism you've written, any response other than an unabashed "Yes!" suggests that your aphorism isn't honest. Reveal yourself without defense. No hiding!

If your goal is to point out that the emperor has no clothes, you must be naked as well. Don't hide behind any -ism or ideology. Don't claim any authority. You are simply sharing what you see to be so. If you need people to agree with you, don't become a holy rascal. If you need people to oppose you, don't become a holy rascal. Holy rascality isn't about you. Holy rascality is about rekindling spiritual creativity and critical thinking. Holy rascality is about freeing the human capacity for religiosity—the capacity for making meaning—from the confines of brand-name religion.

> Aphorisms are not bland generalizations about life, the universe, and everything, but are deeply personal and idiosyncratic statements, as unique to [you] as a strand of [your] DNA.
>
> JAMES GEARY, *The World in a Phrase*

4. Aphorisms Must Have a Twist

Aphorisms must have a twist, a hook, a punch line that catches the reader off guard and throws the reader off balance. Guy Debord called this *détournement*, meaning "turning around." Détournement subverts the memes of the dominant culture by using them to promote alternative messages, creating a sense of cognitive dissonance that causes people to rethink the meaning of conventional wisdom.

Spiritual culture jamming aphorisms pull the rug of certainty out from under the believer, not to mock, but to liberate; not to make fun of religion, but to invite religion to be fun; not to insult belief, but to free the believer for faith. Our goal is to free religion and the religious from stifling literalism by reclaiming myth and metaphor, parable and story as tools for unleashing the imagination in service to wisdom.

If the response to your aphorism is "Duh," you're being too obvious. If the response is, "Huh?" you're being too confusing. If the response is, "Oh!" you're right on target.

Like a good joke, a good aphorism has a punch line, a quick verbal or psychological flip, a sudden sting in the tail that gives you a jolt. Both jokes and aphorisms lift you into a wonderful weightless state—that giddy point just after the joke is finished and just before you get it—then abruptly drop you back down to earth in some completely unexpected place. Aphorisms, like jokes, teach the mind to do the twist.

JAMES GEARY, *The World in a Phrase*

5. Aphorisms Must Be Philosophical

Your aphorisms should be about life: what it is, how to live it, and how to leave it. Aphorisms respond to the big questions: *Who am I? Where did I come from? Where am I going? How should I live?* and *Why?* Spiritually culture jamming aphorisms address the big issues: justice, truth, compassion, love, loss, et cetera. They are not signs pointing to some grand philosophy. They are not blurbs for a book-length discourse. They are not billboards advertising an institution or ideology. They are complete articulations of your wisdom in the moment.

Aphorisms reflect the shifting, scattershot nature of thinking—and the experience of life itself. Aphorisms are "the true form of Universal Philosophy" and contain "the greatest quantity of thought in the smallest space."

FRIEDRICH VON SCHLEGEL,
Dialogue on Poetry and Literary Aphorisms

103
Jaded Wisdom

I call my aphorismic writing Jaded Wisdom. I use the word *jaded* because I offer a satiric read on conventional wisdom. My method is simple: First, I keep my eyes and ears open for spiritual pablum passing as deep wisdom. Second, I quote the original proverb and let my inner satirist add a twist that (I hope) invites the reader to think again about what is being said.

I have written and shared thousands of Jaded Wisdom aphorisms on Twitter and Facebook. The few dozen I offer here are meant to help you get started writing your own.

Jaded Wisdom: Spiritual Proverbs

Each soul has its own reality; each soul has its own truth.
No wonder we're so lonely.

Life is like a box of Cracker Jack: there's a prize inside.
Sure, but it's so cheap that finding it is a waste of time.

Detachment is the key to enlightenment. But who cares?

When you abandon desire, you are gifted with time.
Unfortunately, without desire you'll have nothing to do with it.

Our lives are small; our dreams are great. Live less; sleep more.

Only when you accept yourself as you are can you change.
But then you won't want to.

Behind the clouds the sun is always shining. And behind the
sun is cold, dark, lifeless space. Happy now?

Believe your beliefs, doubt your doubts. And live redundantly
ever after.

Don't be afraid of dumb questions. Be afraid of dumb answers.

Life is a book that never ends. Except that, well, you know,
it does.

Every day is a good day. Though not necessarily for you.

You will always get an idea if you think and don't panic.
Unfortunately, that idea will often be: "Panic!"

The most important thing is to find yourself.
Two steps to finding yourself:
1 Ask yourself where you last saw yourself.
2 Ask yourself whom you are talking to.

What all people have in common is that each one is unique.
So really we have nothing in common at all.

No one owns anything. The sooner you learn this, the sooner
you can start taking whatever you want.

**Some want it to happen, some wish it would happen, some
make it happen.** And some have to clean up after it happens.

When it comes to getting older, we have choices. Not getting older isn't one of them.

When you think positively, your mind becomes a magnet. Stay clear of refrigerators.

Every mistake is a lesson. The lesson is: stop making mistakes.

Learn to love spending time with yourself. After all, it's not like you can leave yourself with a sitter and go out with friends.

Imagine you're already the person you want to be. Then you won't have to bother becoming that person at all.

Wake up each morning believing there's a giant in you; then release it. Don't forget to flush.

Your life is your canvas. Don't be surprised if you've been framed.

Igniting your inner flame is easy. Inserting the candle is a bitch.

Think to yourself: "I choose my thoughts." Now ask yourself: Did I choose to think that thought? Or was I just following orders?

Live your life as if joy were just around the corner. It isn't, but walking around the corner to see is still good exercise.

 In the beginning was the Word. And the Word was with God. And the Word was God. And the Word was trademarked. And the God was branded. And the Word® was lost. And now it's time to reclaim the Word.   RR

Jaded Wisdom: God

Not everyone who worships the dead and risen Lord is a follower of Jesus. Some are followers of Osiris.

Give Satan an inch, and he will become the ruler. Defeat Satan: adopt the metric system.

The last will be first. But only if they can convince the people in front of them that they are facing in the wrong direction.

The pious see more on their knees than the educated can see on their tiptoes. The pious are really, really tall.

God answers prayer with "Yes," "No," and "Wait." If you want more options, try a Magic 8-Ball.

It will cost you more to say no to God than to say yes. But remember: you get what you pay for.

God gave us necks. We invented the noose.

If you believe in God, you cannot be defeated. The motto of religious fanatics everywhere.

God helps those who help themselves. God is redundant.

Go to sleep believing God will take care of tomorrow. But set your alarm just in case.

Some people see more on a walk around the block than others see on a trip around the world. These people live on very long blocks.

Every time God closes a door, he opens a window.
God is claustrophobic.

You can never praise God too much. God's self-esteem is that low.

When God writes "opportunity" on one side of your door, God writes "responsibility" on the other side. God loves vandalizing doors.

Never say, "Tomorrow" when God says, "Today." And don't say, "Tomato" when God says, "Tomahto." In fact, just repeat whatever God says. It's safer that way.

God speaks through your hands. Be careful you aren't worshiping a sock puppet.

Once you are convinced you are doing God's work, all concern with morality is irrelevant.

Some evil is excused by saying, "I was just following orders." The rest is excused by saying, "I was just following God."

In God's eyes, no one is better than anyone else. God needs glasses.

The most important thing is to do your best. Unless your best really sucks. Then the most important thing is to hire someone who can do better.

RR

God is the same yesterday, today, and forever! God is in a rut.

Trees are God's temples. There are so many because God can't decide which one to join.

You are a pencil in the hand of God. If only he'd quit chewing on the end.

God knows exactly the mess you're in. He should. He put you there.

Hard times aren't hurdles on the road to God—they are the road. God, like the rest of us, hates paying for infrastructure repair.

> Feel grateful in this moment. If you don't feel grateful in this moment, be grateful for that, and then you will be grateful in this moment and you can stop worrying about gratitude altogether.   RR

God's Word is like a rest stop on life's highway. Ignore it, and you'll have to wait a few miles before you can pee.

All creatures are words of God. Sadly, some are misspelled.

God gave us two hands, two ears, two eyes, two nostrils, and one mouth. God ran short on mouths.

God doesn't forget the sinner, only the sin. God still punishes you, but he can't remember why.

God says, "Pray for your enemies." "Dear God, please kill my enemies. Amen."

God commands you to love him of your own free will. What is it about *free* that God doesn't understand?

God has a plan for your life. If you woke up miserable this morning, you can assume that's the plan.

> "There but for the grace of God," said John Bradford in the 16th century, on seeing wretches led to execution, "go I." What this apparently compassionate observation really means—not that it really "means" anything—is, "There by the grace of God goes someone else."
>
> CHRISTOPHER HITCHENS, *God Is Not Great*

104
Thou Hast Mail

One of the best holy rascal practices for subverting the presumption of truth at the heart of brand-name religions is to approach them naïvely. Young children do this all the time, but because they are little kids, adults take what they say as cute rather than subversive. "Thou Hast Mail" is just such a practice, seeking to help practitioners imitate the child's naïveté without losing the subversive nature of what is being said by writing faux children's letters to God.

"Thou Hast Mail" is not the same as "Kids Say the Darndest Things," the popular TV and radio feature hosted by Art Linkletter in the 1950s and '60s. Mr. Linkletter asked real questions of real kids. "Thou Hast Mail" is fake because fake is more efficient than real: whereas Mr. Linkletter had to talk with dozens of kids to find one funny one, you can invent the funny kid right off the bat.

When crafting your letters to God, it helps to write them on big eleven-by-fourteen-inch sheets of coloring paper using a large crayon or jumbo-sized marker—anything that feels a bit too large in your hand. In this way you channel your inner child and invite yourself to think differently about theological notions you may have heard all your life. "Thou Hast Mail" is not about dismissing dogma, doctrine, or belief, but about taking dogma, doctrine, and belief to their absurdist conclusions.

Each of the following letters I wrote to God is based on something I heard an adult say in all seriousness.

Thou Hast Mail

Dear God,

My pastor says you need the blood of Jesus to calm down so you won't get mad and send us to Hell. My mom makes me go to my room when I get mad. Maybe you should try that instead.   SAMMI

Dear God,

I'm Jewish and want to apologize for killing your son. I don't remember doing it, but my friends say I did. They also say he came back from the dead, so can we still be friends?   MICAH

Dear God,

When people burn in Hell, do they swell up and turn black like toasted marshmallows? I need to know for my Sunday School exhibit next week.   TIM

Dear God,

My big brother says you are like the Tooth Fairy. So, is the money I give at church the same money you leave under my pillow? If so, you are taking a big cut.   HANNA

Dear God,

My pastor says when your son comes back to earth, he will send my gramma and grampa to Hell because they are Methodists. Please don't let him come back before my birthday because they promised to take me to Disney World.   TONE

Dear God,

My dad keeps telling people to go to Hell, but they never actually go anywhere. I hope you have better luck.   SAUL

Dear God,

If bad people go to Hell and good people go to Heaven, where do better people go?   BRIAN

Dear God,

My friend Hameed says you sent the angel Gabriel to speak to Muhammad. Were you too busy to talk to him yourself?   DARREN

Dear God,

My friend Ram has a picture of you with an elephant head. My dad says it's because you are a Republican.   CYNDI

Dear God,

My big brother says the reason Jesus's tomb was empty is because he donated his body to science. Is this true?   MARIA

Dear God,

My rabbi says you like Israel more than any other country. My teacher is making me write a report on Venezuela. Please don't be mad at me.   ROBERT

Dear God,

I learned today that Mormons wear special underwear. So does my gramma. Do we become Mormons when we get old? JERRY

Dear God,

My grandpa and I used to love baseball, and when he died I put my favorite baseball card in his coffin. I didn't know it was worth lots of money. Could you steal it from him and send it back to me? DEREK

Dear God,

Thanks for not making me live in Bible times. The people had to eat manna, and my mom never lets me eat stuff I find on the ground. I think I'd starve. LYLE

Dear God,

I have a friend who is a Sikh, and he gets to carry a cool sword. My mom won't even let me use scissors. Can you tell her I'm really a Sikh? KERRY

Dear God,

At school I have a Jewish friend who says you want her to cut off her hair when she gets married, and a Sikh friend who says you won't let him cut his hair at all, and a Muslim friend who says you want her to hide her hair under a scarf. What is your problem with hair? NANCI

Dear God,

My dad says you don't want us Jews to turn on our TVs on Saturday, but that we can have a Christian do it for us so we can watch golf. Is he right? Can I have a Christian change the channel to cartoons, or is that not Jewish? GEORGE

Dear God,

My science teacher says dinosaurs died because a huge meteor hit the earth. Did you mean to do that, or were you aiming at something else?   JOEL

Dear God,

We got a new kid in our class today. He's from Mexico. His name is Jesus. Are you related?   MIKE

Dear God,

Before Adam and Eve ate the apple, they were naked and not ashamed. After they ate it, they were naked and ashamed. How many calories were in that apple, anyway?   SALLY

Dear God,

My pastor says you know the future. That must be very boring, like watching reruns without any new shows. I will try and surprise you tomorrow just to help out.   KIM

Dear God,

I read that you killed Job's children to win a bet. My mom has a problem with gambling also. She goes to meetings. Maybe you should try it too.   SARA

Dear God,

If my clothes are left behind at the Rapture, does it matter if I wear clean underwear?   ZANE

Dear God,

I heard that you don't hear the prayers of Jews. Is that because we mumble them?   BERNIE

SCRIPTURES, n. The sacred books of our holy
religion, as distinguished from the false and
profane writings on which all other faiths are based.
Ambrose Bierce, *The Unabridged Devil's Dictionary*

Dear God,

When Mormons knock on our door, we don't answer. When
Jehovah's Witnesses ring the bell, we pretend not to be home.
But when the ice cream truck drives by, we run out to get
some. Maybe you should drive an ice cream truck.   PAUL

Dear God,

My friend Tommy says you are white, but Mrs. Morris next
door says you are every color. I tried coloring you with all my
Crayons, and you ended up black like me. I won't tell Tommy;
he'd be scared to death.   AISHA

105
A Card-Carrying Holy Rascal

One of the simplest hacks you can do is print up small cards with the following message on them and slip them into sacred texts and theology books in bookstores, religious institutions, hotels, hospitals, libraries, et cetera.

> This book contains material on God. God is a matter of belief, beliefs cannot be proven, and the beliefs promoted in this book are only some among many.
>
> Read this book critically and with an open mind. If it leads you to living life more justly and compassionately, learn from it. If not, move on.

Is God serious? And—obviously—the answer is "No."
Alan Watts[19]

106
When All Is Said and Done

Someone hacked the Bible's Book of Ecclesiastes.

After Ecclesiastes (a pseudonym) wrote twelve chapters of largely secular advice on how to live in a world defined by impermanence and insecurity, some editor hacked the book and added, "When all is said and done: fear God and keep His Commandments" (Ecclesiastes 12:13).

Why would someone do this? Perhaps to get the book published? After all, how else would Ecclesiastes's humanistic manifesto make its way into the Holy Bible? Or maybe to sabotage Ecclesiastes's message, undermine his radicalism with a bland affirmation of the status quo.

I mention the hacking of Ecclesiastes because the book you are reading at this moment is also a prime target for hacking. Not by my editor, of course, but by you.

Yes, you, dear reader; you who, while reading this book and test-driving its practices, may have secretly hoped that when all was said and done you could go back to fearing God and keeping his commandments. Well, you can't.

Sure, Dorothy returned to Kansas, but did she return to church? Or if she did, could she passively listen without knowing she was listening to yet another Great and Terrible Wizard? Of course not. Once you've seen the truth, you can't take refuge in ignorance.

But you might want to, and to fulfill that desire you might pretend that this book is saying something it isn't—something safe, conventional, and comfortable; something benign and nonthreatening; something like, "Fear God and keep His commandments." But it isn't.

To prevent any hacking, let me offer this very brief summary of the manifesto you hold in your hands. When all is said and done:

1 Truth is one, different people call it by different names (*Rig-Veda* 1.164.46), and none of them matter. The Tao that can be named is not the eternal Tao (*Tao Te Ching* 1:1).

2 Religions promote names; holy rascals seek Truth.

3 To discover Truth, you must see beyond names.

4 Seeing beyond names, you discover a singular process manifesting reality, as an ocean manifests waves.

5 Discovering this reality in, with, and as all beings, you are called to embrace all beings with respect, justice, and love.

6 Professional clergy may not want you to know this; holy rascals do.

That's it. Don't hack. Be holy.

 What is important is not how to recognize one who is liberated but how to understand yourself. No authority here or hereafter can give you knowledge of yourself; without self-knowledge, there is no liberation from ignorance or sorrow.

J. KRISHNAMURTI, *The Book of Life*

107

How to Avoid the Cross, the Stake, Stoning, and Beheading

You can't.

Jesus said, "Take up your cross, and follow me" (Matthew 16:24). Before signing up to do this, you might want to ask Jesus where he's going. The answer is Calvary, the place of crucifixion. That's why you need your cross. If he was going to the mall, he would have told you to take your credit card. But he didn't, because he isn't. And because credit cards hadn't been invented yet, though he must have known about them because he is God and God knows everything.

Following Jesus, one of the greatest holy rascals who ever lived, means being a holy rascal. Following Jesus and being a holy rascal is to stand against the powers that be and proclaim the emperor has no clothes. And he doesn't. But he has lots of fanatics whose primary job is to silence you. In the old days, the preferred methods of silencing were crucifixion, burning at the stake, stoning, and beheading. Today it's mostly beheading. And Internet trolling.

Rules are made to be broken.
Whoever said that didn't make the rules.

RR

While the apostle John was right that "the truth will set you free" (John 8:32), what he failed to add was that sharing the truth might get you dead. But hey, what's life without a little risk? And pulling the curtain back on the Great and Terrible Wizard is a lot more fun than jumping off a mountain in a wing suit. Or so I've been told.

Anyway, if you want to keep your head, never raise it up. If you want to fit in, never stand up. If you want to keep your voice, never speak the truth.

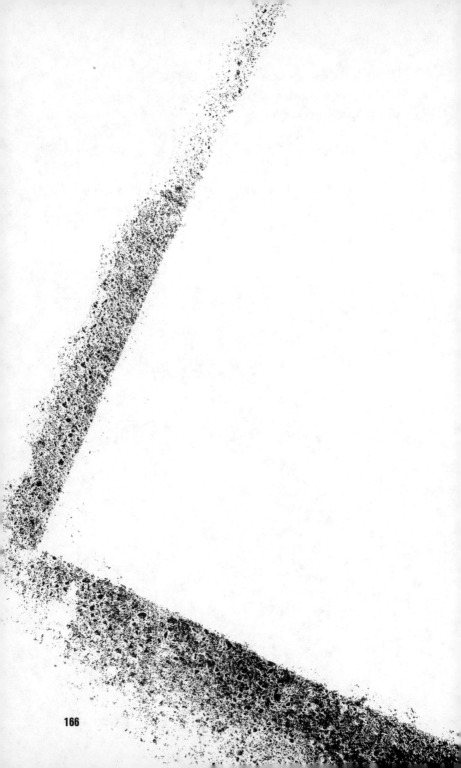

108

EPILOGUE
There's a God at the End
of This Book!

WHOA!

Do you know there's a God at the end of this book?

If I were you, I'd

PUT THIS BOOK DOWN RIGHT NOW.

Gods are not good.

Gods are not nice.

Gods are scary, and the last thing you

want to do is run into one of them.

So be smart and close this book and put it down.

Now!

SERIOUSLY?

YOU TURNED THE PAGE?

DID YOU KNOW THAT ONCE GOD

GOT SO MAD AT PEOPLE, HE DROWNED THEM ALL?

EVERY WOMAN, CHILD, AND MAN—

INNOCENT AND GUILTY ALIKE.

AND THEN, JUST TO BE SAFE,

HE KILLED ALMOST ALL THE ANIMALS AND BIRDS

AND FISH AND EVERYTHING.

THIS GUY'S FREAKY. HE CAN DROWN FISH!

PLUS HE TURNED OVER WHAT WAS LEFT

TO AN ALCOHOLIC NAMED NOAH.

HE'S CLEARLY WACK-A-DOO.

SO PLEASE DO NOT TURN THE PAGE!

ARE YOU NUTS!?
DIDN'T YOU HEAR WHAT I SAID?
THERE'S A GOD
AT THE END OF THIS BOOK!
LISTEN, I'M NOT KIDDING.
AFTER HE DROWNED EVERYONE, HE LET PEOPLE MULTIPLY AND
THEN CHOSE ABE AND SARAH TO BE HIS BEST BUDS.
GOD PROMISED THEM A KID, AND THEY HAD ONE,
AND THEN GOD ORDERED ABE TO MURDER HIM
JUST TO SEE IF ABE LOVED GOD MORE THAN HE LOVED HIS SON!
THIS IS NOT SOMEBODY YOU WANT TO MESS WITH.
SO PLEASE,
DO NOT TURN THE PAGE!

AHHH!

You turned the page!

Don't you believe me?

I'm not making this up.

Listen, after Abe, God's people were enslaved in Egypt,

and there was this fellow Moses

who worked for God and got them out.

But God tortured the Egyptians first. Why?

To show them who's Boss, that's why.

He sent his Angel of Death to kill

every firstborn male in Egypt.

Why? 'Cause he could, that's why.

You do not want to meet this God!

SO PLEASE:
DO NOT TURN THE PAGE!

OK! NOW I'M SCARED!

Maybe you think you can bargain with God,

is that it? You think you can kiss up to him?

Let me tell you something.

His high priest Aaron had two boys

who loved God so much they wanted to worship him.

Their names were Nadab and Abihu.

No, you wouldn't want to go through school

with those names today, but that wasn't their problem.

Their problem was that they loved God

and went to worship him but did so in the wrong way.

So you know what God did?

He burned them up like toast!

Why? 'Cause he's nuts, that's why!

So come on, whaddya say, don't turn the page?

DO YOU HAVE
A DEATH WISH?
MAYBE YOU THINK ANOTHER GOD WILL SAVE YOU.
IS THAT IT? WELL, FORGET THAT!
THERE WAS A GOD NAMED BAAL
WHO CHALLENGED GOD AND
SO GOD'S PROPHET ELIJAH CHALLENGED
THE PRIESTS OF BAAL TO A FIRE-MAKING CONTEST.
TWO HUNDRED AND FIFTY OF BAAL'S GUYS AGAINST ELIJAH.
THE BAAL BOYS PRAYED AND PRAYED,
BUT THEIR GOD DIDN'T EVEN GIVE 'EM A SPARK.
ELIJAH CALLED TO HIS GOD, AND WHAMMM!
NOT ONLY DID THE FIRE IGNITE,
BUT THE 250 PRIESTS OF BAAL CAUGHT FIRE
ALONG WITH IT.
DON'T TURN THE PAGE!

STOP TURNING PAGES!

MAYBE YOU'RE A KID

AND YOU THINK GOD WON'T KILL KIDS.

BUT HE DOES.

THAT PROPHET ELIJAH I MENTIONED?

ONCE THERE WERE FORTY-TWO KIDS MAKING FUN OF HIM,

AND HE CALLED OUT TO GOD,

AND YOU KNOW WHAT GOD DID?

HE SENT A HUGE BEAR TO KILL THE KIDS.

NOT SCARE 'EM AWAY—*KILL THEM!*

GOD'S GOT A THING FOR KILLING KIDS.

SO PLEASE—
DO NOT TURN THE PAGE!

WILL NOTHING STOP YOU?

No one is safe from God.

There was this fella Job—nicest guy, loved God—

and God killed his kids and his servants.

Why?

'Cause God bet the Devil that Job wouldn't get mad.

That's right: God murdered Job's kids

just to see if that would piss Job off.

And when it didn't,

God tortured Job and covered his body in oozing sores.

Sure, God healed Job and gave him new kids

when still Job refused to get mad,

but all the same, this isn't the act of a sane person.

SO PLEASE
DO NOT TURN THE PAGE!

ARE YOU MAD?

YOU ARE ALMOST THERE!

ONE LAST TRY:

THIS GOD IS SO NUTS HE KILLED HIS OWN KID.

HE HAD A BABY BOY WITH A JEWISH GIRL,

AND HE SET HIM AGAINST ROME,

AND THE ROMANS CRUCIFIED HIM.

THAT'S WHAT HE DID. HE HAD HIS OWN SON MURDERED.

HE COULD HAVE STOPPED IT. BUT HE DIDN'T.

SOME PEOPLE SAY HIS SON IS GOD, TOO.

AND THEN YOU KNOW WHAT GOD DOES?

HE COMES BACK AND SLAUGHTERS MILLIONS MORE PEOPLE!

PLEASE PLEASE PLEASE
DO NOT TURN THE PAGE!

OK! I SEE YOU ARE DETERMINED
TO MEET THIS GOD. WELL, GO
AHEAD THEN, TURN THE PAGE AND
SEE WHO IT IS THAT SLAUGHTERS
MILLIONS. I TRIED TO SAVE YOU,
BUT IT'S YOUR FUNERAL.
TURN THE DAMN PAGE!

Acknowledgments

Like raising a child, it takes a village to write a book. When contemplating the writing of this book I expected to return to the same village I hired to raise my son, a small hamlet in darkest Nova Scotia, but they were busy and said that raising a boy and writing a book are two very different enterprises, and so they passed on my offer. My second choice, and one most amenable to the writing of this book, was the village of Sounds True. Let me tell you why.

First, the dogs. The village of Sounds True is not simply dog friendly, but dog dominated. You can't tell whether the people bring their canine friends to work or it is the canines who bring their human friends to work. In either case, if you ever go to visit, don't wear black.

Second, the people. Maybe it's the dogs, maybe it's the mountains, maybe it's something in the water, but the people at Sounds True are so kind, generous, and loving that after only a short visit I wanted to work there. Well, not work exactly, just sort of hang out like the dogs with my own mat and water bowl.

It was my agent, Scott Edelstein, who convinced Sounds True to take me on. This is Scott's fifth project with me. The first four are in Polish, so you may not have seen them. In any case, thanks, Scott. And thanks as well to Jennifer Brown, who was brave enough to acquire the book for Sounds True.

My son Aaron was my first reader. As a professor of writing and literature, he helped me with the former and continually reminded me that this was not even close to the latter. Thanks, boy.

My book editor at Sounds True was Gretel Hakanson. I'm not sure she or the Sounds True family knew what to expect from this book. But she and they were open to almost anything. Gretel did a marvelous job making this book as playful in form as print allows. I am grateful for her creativity, skill, rascality, and willingness to play along.

This book has a companion audio program. Mitchell Clute was the editor of my nine-hour stream-of-consciousness dive into the wilds of religion and holy rascality. He just had me sit in a stuffed chair covered in dog hair (yes, I wore black!), fitted me with headphones and a mic, and told me to start talking. He trusted the universe that something worth listening to would come out of these sessions. I trusted him to help the universe along. This book is not a transcript of the audio series, so feel free to purchase both without fear that you are acting redundantly.

Lastly, a few words about Sounds True's founder and publisher, Tami Simon. She is a woman of deep wisdom and integrity who has managed to create a company that mirrors her values. I have known Tami for a long time and have yearned to publish with Sounds True even longer. It took me two decades to finally come up with an idea she found compelling. I've forgotten what it is, but the fact that she agreed to publish this project proves that if you are willing to wave your arms like an inflatable air dancer for decades, you too might at last have a chance to say, "I publish with Sounds True." Now if someone would plug me back in, I'd like to pitch her on another idea.

Notes

1 Joshu Sasaki Roshi, interview by Ralph Blumenthal, *New York Times*, December 9, 2007.

2 Ibid.

3 Abraham Abulafia, thirteenth-century Kabbalist, quoted in Moshe Idel's *The Mystical Experience of Abraham Abulafia*.

4 Ramakrishna, *The Gospel of Sri Ramakrishna*, trans. Swami Nikhilananda (New York: Ramakrishna-Vivekananda Center, 2007).

5 J. Krishnamurti, public talk in Brockwood Park School, Hampshire, England, September 7, 1980.

6 Lucius Annaeus Seneca, *Epistles*, trans. Richard M. Gummere (Cambridge, MA: Harvard University Press, 1920).

7 Martin Buber, *I and Thou* (New York: Touchstone, 1970), 61.

8 Gene Roddenberry, interview by David Alexander, *The Humanist*. (March/April 1991).

9 Karen Armstrong, interview by Terry Gross, *Fresh Air*, NPR, September 21, 2009.

10 *The Forward* and Daniel Estrin, "The King's Torah: A Rabbinic Text or a Call to Terror?," *Haaretz*, January 22, 2010.

11 Steven Weinberg, "A Designer Universe?," address at the Conference on Cosmic Design, American Association for the Advancement of Science, Washington, DC, April 1999.

12 Gonzalo Fernández de Oviedo, *Historia general y natural de las Indias, islas y tierra-firme del mar océano.* (Charleston, SC: Nabu Press, 2014).

13 Karen Armstrong, quoted in Jay Sidebotham's *Conversations with Scripture: Romans* (New York: Morehouse Publishing, 2015).

14 Alan Watts, *Does It Matter?: Essays on Man's Relation to Materiality* (New York: New World Library, 2007), 60.

15 Karen Armstrong, interview by Terry Gross, *Fresh Air*, NPR, September 21, 2009.

16 Czeslaw Milosz, Nobel Prize lecture, Stockholm, Sweden, December 8, 1980.

17 James Geary, *The World in a Phrase: A Brief History of the Aphorism* (New York: Bloomsbury, 2005), 9.

18 Ibid., 15–16.

19 Alan Watts, *Out of Your Mind: Tricksters, Interdependence, and the Cosmic Game of Hide and Seek* (Boulder, CO: Sounds True, 2017).

Bibliography

Alexander, David. "*The Humanist* Interview with Gene Roddenberry." *The Humanist*, March/April 1991.

Aquinas, Saint Thomas. *Selected Writings*. New York: Penguin Putnam, 1998.

Armstrong, Karen. *The Great Transformation*. New York: Anchor Books, 2007.

_____. Interview by Bill Moyers, *NOW with Bill Moyers*, PBS, March 1, 2002.

_____. Interview by Terry Gross, *Fresh Air*, NPR, September 21, 2009.

Augustine. *The Literal Meaning of Genesis*. Vol. 1. Edited by Johannes Quasten, Walter Burghardt, and Thomas Lawler. Mahwah, NJ: Paulist Press, 1982.

Baldwin, James. *The Fire Next Time*. New York: Vintage, 1993.

Berman, Morris. *Twilight of American Culture*. New York: W. W. Norton, 2000.

Bierce, Ambrose. *The Unabridged Devil's Dictionary*. New York: Dover, 1993.

Blumenthal, Ralph. "A Very Old Zen Master and His Art of Tough Love." *New York Times*, December 9, 2007.

Bowen, Jack. *If You Can Read This: The Philosophy of Bumper Stickers*. New York: Random House, 2010.

Bruce, Steve. "Authority and Freedom: Economics and Secularization." In *Religions as Brands: New Perspectives on the Marketization of Religion and Spirituality*, edited by Jean-Claude Usunier and Jörg Stolz, 91–204. Burlington, VT: Ashgate Publishing, 2014.

Buber, Martin. *I and Thou*. New York: Touchstone, 1970.

Buechner, Frederick. *Telling the Truth: The Gospel as Tragedy, Comedy, and Fairy Tale*. New York: HarperCollins, 1977.

Campbell, Joseph. *The Power of Myth*. New York: Anchor Books, 1988.

Chapman, Graham, John Cleese, Terry Gilliam, Eric Idle, Terry Jones, and Michael Palin. *Monty Python's Life of Brian*. Directed by Terry Jones. London: HandMade Films, 1979. 94 min.

Debord, Guy. *The Society of the Spectacle*. New York: Zone Books, 1995.

de Montfort, Louis. *The Secret of Mary*. Bay Shore, NY: Montfort Publications, 2013.

Eagleton, Terry. *Why Marx Was Right*. New Haven, CT: Yale University Press, 2011.

Eco, Umberto. *The Name of the Rose*. New York: Harcourt, 1980.

Einstein, Albert. *Ideas and Opinions*. New York: Crown Publishers, 1982.

Fernández de Oviedo, Gonzalo. *Historia general y natural de las Indias, islas y tierra-firme del mar océano*. Charleston, SC: Nabu Press, 2014.

Feuerbach, Ludwig. *The Essence of Christianity*. Amherst, NY: Prometheus Books, 1989.

The Forward and Daniel Estrin, "The King's Torah: A Rabbinic Text or a Call to Terror?" *Haaretz*, January 22, 2010. http://www.haaretz.com /jewish/news/the-king-s-torah-a-rabbinic-text-or-a-call-to-terror -1.261930.

Geary, James. *Geary's Guide to the World's Great Aphorists*. New York: Bloomsbury, 2007.

———. *The World in a Phrase: A Brief History of the Aphorism*. New York: Bloomsbury, 2005.

Gladwell, Malcom. *The Tipping Point*. New York: Little, Brown, 2000.

Gordon, Mordechai. *Humor, Laughter, and Human Flourishing: A Philosophical Exploration of the Laughing Animal*. New York: Springer, 2014.

Gross, John. *The Oxford Book of Aphorisms*. New York: Oxford University Press, 1983.

Harris, Sam. *Letter to a Christian Nation*. New York: Vintage Books, 2008.

Harvey, Andrew. *The Return of the Mother*. New York: Tarcher, 2000.

Havens, Teresina. *Mind What Stirs in Your Heart*. Wallingford, PA: Pendle Hill Publications, 2015.

Heath, Dan, and Chip Heath. *Made to Stick*. New York: Random House, 2008.

Herbert, Frank. *Dune*. New York: Penguin Books, 2016.

His Holiness the Dalai Lama. *Ethics for the New Millennium*. New York: Riverhead Books, 1999.

Hitchens, Christopher. *God Is Not Great: How Religion Poisons Everything*. New York: Hachette, 2007.

Hobday, Jose. *Stories of Awe and Abundance*. New York: Continuum International, 1995.

Huizinga, Johan. *Homo Ludens: A Study of the Play-Element in Culture*. Kettering, OH: Angelico Press, 2016.

Hyde, Lewis. *Trickster Makes This World*. New York: North Point Press, 1998.

Idel, Moshe. *The Mystical Experience of Abraham Abulafia*. Albany, NY: SUNY Press, 1988.

Kafka, Franz. *Parable and Paradox*. New York: Schocken Books, 1961.

Kaplan, Mordecai. *Judaism as a Civilization: Toward a Reconstruction of American-Jewish Life*. New York: Jewish Publication Society, 2010.

Keating, Thomas. *Manifesting God*. New York: Lantern Books, 2005.

Kesey, Ken. *Kesey's Garage Sale*. New York: Viking Press, 1973.

Klein, Naomi. *No Logo*. New York: Picador, 2002.

Kramer, Kenneth Paul. *Learning through Dialogue: The Relevance of Martin Buber's Classroom*. Lanham, MD: Rowman & Littlefield, 2013.

Krishnamurti, J. *The Book of Life: Daily Meditations with Krishnamurti*. Edited by Mark Lee. New York: HarperCollins, 1995.

_____. Public talk in Brockwood Park School, Hampshire, England, September 7, 1980.

Lakoff, George. *Don't Think of an Elephant*. White River Junction, VT: Chelsea Green, 2004.

Lasn, Kalle. *Culture Jam*. New York: HarperCollins, 2000.

———. *Design Anarchy*. New York: ORO Editions, 2006.

———. *Meme Wars*. New York: Seven Stories Press, 2012.

Levinson, Jay Conrad. *Guerrilla Creativity*. Boston: Houghton Mifflin, 2001.

Maher, Bill. *Religulous*. Directed by Larry Charles. Los Angeles: Thousand Words, 2008. 101 min.

Marmysz, John. *Laughing at Nothing: Humor as a Response to Nihilism*. Albany, NY: SUNY Press, 2003.

Miller, Anne. *Metaphorically Selling*. New York: Chiron Associates, 2004.

Milosz, Czeslaw. Nobel Prize lecture, Stockholm, Sweden, December 8, 1980.

Morreall, John. *Comic Relief: A Comprehensive Philosophy of Humor*. New York: Wiley-Blackwell, 2009.

———. *The Philosophy of Laughter and Humor*. Albany, NY: SUNY Press, 1986.

Morson, Gary Saul. *The Long and Short of It: From Aphorism to Novel*. Stanford, CA: Stanford University Press, 2012.

Patai, Raphael. *The Hebrew Goddess*. Detroit: Wayne State University Press, 1990.

Postman, Neil. *Amusing Ourselves to Death*. New York: Penguin Books, 1986.

Ramakrishna. *The Gospel of Sri Ramakrishna*. Translated by Swami Nikhilananda. New York: Ramakrishna-Vivekananda Center, 2005.

Rivkin, Ellis. *The Dynamics of Jewish History*. Sarasota, FL: New College, 1970.

Sagaolla, Dom. *140 Characters: A Style Guide for the Short Form*. Hoboken, NJ: Wiley & Sons, 2009.

Schachter-Shalomi, Zalman. *Paradigm Shift: From the Jewish Renewal Teachings of Reb Zalman Schachter-Shalomi*. Lanham, MD: Jason Aronson, 2000.

_____. *Wrapped in a Holy Flame*. Hoboken, NJ: Josey-Bass, 2003.

Schopenhauer, Arthur. *The World as Will and Representation*. London: Kegan Paul, Trench, Trubner, 1909.

_____. *Essays and Aphorisms*. New York: Penguin Books, 1970.

Seneca, Lucius Annaeus. *Epistles*. Translated by Richard M. Gummere. Cambridge, MA: Harvard University Press, 1920.

Sidebotham, Jay. *Conversations with Scripture: Romans*. New York: Morehouse Publishing, 2015.

Smith, Huston. *The World's Religions*. New York: HarperOne, 1991.

Stolz, Jörg, and Jean-Claude Usunier, eds. *Religions as Brands: New Perspectives on the Marketization of Religion and Spirituality*. Burlington, VT: Ashgate Publishing, 2014.

Twain, Mark. *The Wit and Wisdom of Mark Twain*. Philadelphia: Running Press, 2002.

Unno, Taitetsu. *Shin Buddhism: Bits of Rubble Turned into Gold*. New York: Harmony Books, 2002.

Voas, David. "Preface." In *Religions as Brands: New Perspectives on the Marketization of Religion and Spirituality*, edited by Jean-Claude Usunier and Jörg Stolz, xvii–xix. Burlington, VT: Ashgate Publishing, 2014.

von Schlegel, Friedrich. *Dialogue on Poetry and Literary Aphorisms*. Translated by Ernst Behler and Roman Struc. University Park, PA: Pennsylvania University Press, 1967.

Watts, Alan. *The Book on the Taboo against Knowing Who You Are*. New York: Random House, 1999.

_____. *Does It Matter?: Essays on Man's Relation to Materiality*. New York: New World Library, 2007.

_____. *Out of Your Mind: Tricksters, Interdependence, and the Cosmic Game of Hide and Seek*. Boulder, CO: Sounds True, 2017.

Weil, Simone. *Gravity and Grace*. New York: Routledge, 1999.

_____. *Selected Essays, 1934–1943*. Eugene, OR: Wipf and Stock Publishers, 1962.

Weinberg, Steven. "A Designer Universe?" Address at the Conference on Cosmic Design, American Association for the Advancement of Science, Washington, DC, April 1999.

Whitman, Walt. *Walt Whitman's Camden Conversations*. New Brunswick, NJ: Rutgers University Press, 1973.

Wilber, Ken. *The Simple Feeling of Being*. Boston: Shambhala, 2004.

About the Author

I was born of a human mother on April 26, 1951. My mother was born of a mother from the same species some twenty-one years earlier. My mother's mother has a similar origin, and this goes back awhile until we get to my great grandmother, who was an ape. She too came from a mother, and as best I can tell, it is mothers all the way down to the original Virgin Birth: the Big Bang some 13.8 billion years ago.

I'm a late bloomer and didn't do much for most of these 13.8 billion years, but in the last four decades I managed to earn rabbinic ordination from Hebrew Union College and a PhD from Union Graduate School, create a synagogue, work as a management consultant for Fortune 500 companies, teach Comparative Religion at Middle Tennessee State University, author the Roadside Assistance for the Spiritual Traveler column for *Spirituality & Health* magazine, host the magazine's weekly podcast, *Essential Conversations with Rabbi Rami*, found the One River Foundation, get initiated into the Ramakrishna Order of Vedanta Hinduism, and publish some thirty or so books. Today I am a freelance holy rascal making my living writing and talking. I know, I can't believe it either.

About Sounds True

Sounds True is a multimedia publisher whose mission is to inspire and support personal transformation and spiritual awakening. Founded in 1985 and located in Boulder, Colorado, we work with many of the leading spiritual teachers, thinkers, healers, and visionary artists of our time. We strive with every title to preserve the essential "living wisdom" of the author or artist. It is our goal to create products that not only provide information to a reader or listener, but that also embody the quality of a wisdom transmission.

For those seeking genuine transformation, Sounds True is your trusted partner. At SoundsTrue.com you will find a wealth of free resources to support your journey, including exclusive weekly audio interviews, free downloads, interactive learning tools, and other special savings on all our titles.

To learn more, please visit SoundsTrue.com/freegifts or call us toll-free at 800.333.9185.

SOUNDS TRUE
many voices, one journey